CHRISTIANITY IS
JEWISH

Christianity

EDITH
SCHAEFFER

Is ***JEWISH***

TYNDALE
House Publishers, Inc.
Wheaton, Illinois

Visit Tyndale's exciting Web site at www.tyndale.com

Library of Congress Catalog Card Number 75-7224
ISBN 8423-0242-5, paper
Printed in the United States of America

05 04 03
27 26 25 24 23

CONTENTS

ONE

The warmth and glow of a wood fire burning in a stone fireplace
drew my husband and me toward the closest two chairs where
we could stretch out our chilled legs and shiver with delight
in the smoke-fragrant contrast to the cold drizzle in which we
had been hiking. It had been fun, of a sort, escaping from the
porcupine which had been nosing around our sleeping bag, and
sleeping on the hard iron slats of the top of a fire tower the
night before, but this was a much more luxurious way to get out
of the rain! We were looking forward to a wonderful alone
evening this rare moment of being away on a short hiking
vacation, away from studies and our precious first baby,
away for a very brief "second honeymoon." It was Bear
Mountain Inn on the Hudson River, and the year was 1937.

A few minutes later we realized that after all this was not a
private lodge, but an inn indeed, as another couple hesitated
at the doorway, and then resolutely crossed over, greeted us,
and drew up chairs. "Nice fire." "Yes, great on a rainy evening."
"Where are you from?"

Should we stay and talk? Should we go to our room and
read? The fire put off a decision ... and before long we were
deep in a conversation which lasted until after midnight. You see,
the man was a Jewish newspaper reporter, who was one day to
become a very well-known Labor reporter, and a question he
asked early in our conversation arrested us, and gave us a deep
desire for a really honest discussion. "When I look at my beautiful

curly-headed three-year-old boy asleep in his crib, I
ask ... why, *why,* does he have to be Jewish? Why can't he be
just a plain American after three generations? What is a Jew
anyway? Why does he have to be always a Jew?"

It was a double-sided question asking not only what is a Jew,
but what is the source of anti-Semitism.

We talked about Adam and Eve, about Cain and Abel, about
Abraham and Moses, about David and Isaiah. We talked about
the God of Isaac, Jacob, and Joseph. The fire burned
low ... and our discussion continued, warm, vivid, real
communication. As we stood up our new Jewish friend said, "I
want to quote you a poem, author unknown, which is a great way
of expressing my own past puzzle about things."

> *How odd of God*
> *To choose the Jew,*
> *But not so odd*
> *As those who choose*
> *The Jewish God*
> *And hate the Jew.*

It was in Saint Louis, Missouri, ten years later in 1947, when I
was asked by a ladies society to give a talk on the Day of
Atonement. Looking into Leviticus I read, "And Aaron
shall offer his bullock of the sin offering, which is for himself,
and make an atonement for himself, and for his house... And he
shall put the incense upon the fire before the Lord, that the
cloud of the incense may cover the mercy seat that is upon
the testimony, that he die not: And he shall take of the blood of
the bullock, and sprinkle it with his finger upon the mercy seat
eastward; and before the mercy seat shall he sprinkle of the
blood with his finger seven times.... And there shall be no
man in the tabernacle of the congregation when he goeth in to
make an atonement in the holy place, until he come out, and have
made an atonement for himself, and for his household, and for
all the congregation of Israel."

"I wonder," I thought, "what the Day of Atonement means
to the Jew today?" My next thought rapidly followed this, "I think
I'll go to some houses in our neighborhood and try to make a

ONE

little research for my paper on The Atonement." My closest neighbor was a bit taken aback at my question. "Gosh, I don't know really ... I mean I guess it is something like the Passover. The Passover was when the Jews passed over the Red Sea, wasn't it? I don't go to the Synagogue myself. Gee, I don't really know anything about it. Why don't you go back on Pershing Avenue to number ---; there's a dentist there who could tell you more about it. He's a good Jew."

As a tall, dark-haired lady opened the door I felt a bit embarrassed but I explained quickly, "I'm writing a paper I have to present, on The Day of Atonement, and in addition to seeing what the Old Testament has to say about it, I would like to find out what The Day of Atonement means to Jews today. I hope it won't inconvenience you right now to tell me what this means to you."

"Come on in," she said cordially. "I'll get papa to talk to you. He really knows more about it than I do."

Soon an older grey-haired man with slightly stooped shoulders came down the stairs, and greeted me kindly. As he heard my question, he sat down where he was, halfway down the last curve of the wide stairs, and with a far-away look in his eyes began to talk gently. He talked of his boyhood in Austria and told of his father and grandfather. He remembered out loud as his eyes seemed to look back through the years rather than seeing me. He told of the anticipation of that Day of Atonement as each one—and the boy who had been himself—tried to remember his sins through the year and to be sorry for them one by one. He told of what it felt like to fast and to do no work that day. He touched his lips with his tongue in remembrance as he said, "We fasted properly, we drank no water, we did not even clean our teeth that day."

As he came to the end of his tale of remembrance of those past years, and then brought his own thoughts up to date, I thanked him with really deep appreciation for having taken the time and care to tell me so completely what I had wanted to know. Then suddenly his daughter asked, "Please, would you tell me what makes your attitude so different from most Gentiles I have met? You are so warm and I feel a love for us in your attitude. What is it that makes you love us? I can feel it ... and I want to know why."

I took a deep breath as I hesitated to answer, and then said, "If you *really* want to know, if you aren't asking for a superficial answer but the real one, I would need to take a long time in answering. I would need to give you a bird's-eye view of the Bible. I have just come into your home with a question which your father has wonderfully answered. I don't want to presume upon your hospitality to tell you something you may not want to hear. I don't want to thrust upon you something which might seem offensive to you, having not really been invited in the first place. Do you see what I mean? So, tell me whether you want me to go into my complete and very long story of why I really do love Jews, why I think it should be natural to anyone who takes the Bible seriously to love Jews."

She now turned to her father and asked, "Papa, we would like to hear it all, wouldn't we?" And he replied very seriously, "Yes, daughter, we would."

And so I sat down on the bottom step of the stairs, and the daughter sat down on the step just above her father ... and completely oblivious of the fact that it was a strange place to spend an evening, the three of us were soon involved in a togetherness of considering what the Bible's central teaching was as the bird's-eye view unfolded. As I got to the place of needing to continue into the New Testament, I stopped again to be sure I would not offend. "Do you want me to go on? I don't want to speak of things which would offend you."

"Go on ... please go on ... don't stop," came the reply. So I continued, right through to the end of Revelation and all that is pictured ahead.

When I finished, and the heavenly city had been described, and the whole story had come to its climax, the old Austrian Jew sighed a deep sigh, and turning his head to look up at his daughter said, "Daughter, have you *ever* heard anything so beautiful?"

"No, Father, I never have."

Then the father turned his head to look down at me. "For thirty years I have been a dentist in this city. For thirty years I have had Gentile patients. *Why* has no one ever told me all this before?"

It was a Sunday afternoon in 1960. L'Abri was now five years old. We had been living in this Swiss Alpine village for five years now, receiving and talking to a tremendous diversity of people. This particular afternoon a Jewish international reporter, the foreign news editor of a prominent news magazine, was sitting beside me on the red couch in the Chalet living room. He was spending a day at L'Abri as a kind of "thank you" to us for what we had done to help his daughter during the last few weeks of her time at a nearby boarding school. Dinner had been a bit of an embarrassment to him, as having a blessing before a meal was obviously not the custom in the Paris international writers' set! Conversation was a bit out of his realm too. Finally after dessert and coffee he had followed me down to the living room to talk. His first question was a reporter's desire for information. "Tell me, what is it you believe. Is this a new religion?"

And so I began to tell the bird's-eye view of the Bible once more, by way of explanation. "This is going to be a full answer," I cautioned him. "It may take all afternoon. But if you really want to know, it would be foolish for me to give you a superficial reply."

Two hours later he sighed, as my voice stopped at the obvious end of the tale. "And what do you call this religion?" he asked—and then he went on immediately a bit defiantly, as well as *wonderingly*, to say, "It sounds like a *Jewish* religion to me."

"Yes," I replied firmly, "Christianity *is Jewish*." I went on to say that I felt that the twisted, warped idea that Christians should be anti-Semitic was a horrible travesty on truth. Christianity is meant to be Jewish. That is what it is all about. Christians ought to love Jews.

Years before, my husband and I had been walking down Columbus Circle in New York on a cold and windy afternoon. Suddenly we came to a place where a man was literally standing on a soap box, having a hard time as he rather loudly preached a rather simple gospel message. We stood

nearby to listen for awhile and nodded our encouragement,
as we felt a bit sorry for him. In a flash as he felt he had some
support, the man had jumped down and asked my husband to say
a few words, which he did, and then I felt myself being lifted up
on the soap box. It was the first and last time I have stood on
a soap box before a crowd of curious-eyed men, some with a bit
of a sneer. These were New York Jews who had stopped before
going on in their walk from one place to another to listen to
whatever was being said from this makeshift platform.

What could I say? This flashed into my mind: "One of the
early Christians, a Jew named Paul, said to the Hebrews as he
wrote a letter to the Corinthians, 'Are they Hebrews? so am
I ... Are they Israelites? so am I. Are they seed of Abraham?
so am I.'

"This same Paul as he spoke to Gentiles warned them. He had
been explaining to them that the Jewish people could be
described as a tree with many branches. This tree was the
true Olive tree, made up of the chosen people, chosen by God
in Abraham to whom the promise was given and with whom a
covenant was made. Because of unbelief—that is, because of
not believing God—branches of the natural olive tree were
broken off. However, Paul said, branches from a wild olive
tree were grafted in to these broken-off places. You Gentiles,
when you believed, were grafted into the true tree, but you
came from a wild olive tree. How can you possibly boast or
be proud of your place? 'Don't boast,' says Paul. 'Don't boast
against the broken-off branches just because you are in the tree.'
If God cuts off natural branches because of unbelief, He won't
spare the wild branches if they don't believe. And in addition to
this, if the *natural* branches which have been cut off because of
unbelief, then come to believe, don't you think God will graft
them back in even more into their own olive tree? Don't be
stupidly blind, you who have been delivered from death because
of the fulfillment of a promise given to the chosen people Israel.
Someday you will see Israel turning back to God in belief.
Some day very, very many of the natural branches will be back
in the true olive tree where they belong."

How different history might have been if Gentile Christians

ONE

had heeded the Jewish Paul's warning ... how different if
people wearing the label "Christian" had all been *real*.

Back again in 1947 I had been invited for a second evening of
conversation with the Austrian Jewish dentist and his
daughter, this time with my Bible, to answer some
questions. With a Bible open on my lap, engrossed in
answering questions, I noticed out of the corner of my eye a
stream of university-age fellows passing the arched doorway.
"My son's fraternity meeting is here tonight," explained the
man's daughter.

Soon the son came to the arched opening into the hall, and
leaned against a post. He was trying to ask some catch
questions concerning the Bible, which I carefully answered,
and two other fellows were there to see the results. After a
time I said, "Now I've been answering questions, I'd like to ask
you one, if you don't mind."

"Sure, go ahead."

"I'm going to read you a passage from one of your Jewish
prophets, Isaiah, who lived seven hundred years before Jesus was
born. Remember now, this was written seven hundred years
before the birth of Christ."

Then I read: "He is despised and rejected of men; a man of
sorrows and acquainted with grief: and we hid as it were our faces
from him; he was despised and we esteemed him not. Surely he
hath borne our griefs, and carried our sorrows: yet we did
esteem him stricken, smitten of God, and afflicted. But he was
wounded for our transgressions, he was bruised for our iniquities:
the chastisement of our peace was upon him; and with his
stripes we are healed. All we like sheep have gone astray; we
have turned every one to his own way; and the Lord has laid
upon him the iniquity of us all. He was oppressed, and he was
afflicted, yet he opened not his mouth: he is brought as a lamb
to the slaughter, and as a sheep before her shearers is dumb,
so he openeth not his mouth. He was taken from prison and
from judgment: and who shall declare his generation? for he was
cut off out of the land of the living: for the transgression of my
people was he stricken. And he made his grave with the
wicked, and with the rich in his death; because he had done no

violence, neither was there any deceit in his mouth. Yet it pleased the Lord to bruise him; he hath put him to grief:... He shall see of the travail of his soul, and shall be satisfied: by his knowledge shall my righteous servant justify many; for he shall bear their iniquities. He bare the sin of many, and made intercession for the transgressors."

"Who was Isaiah referring to?

The student gave a little snort, an impatient scornful kind of laugh, "Huh, that's easy; that is a description of Jesus Christ."

In the moment of electric silence which followed this outburst I said with amazement, "Do you realize what you have just said? Don't forget I was fair to you in prefacing what I read with telling you it was written seven hundred years before Christ was born."

All three boys sat down as if someone had hit them with a violent blow, this son of the household with his head buried in his hands. Suddenly he looked up at me and said accusingly, "Tell me then *why* the Jews don't accept this Jesus Christ as the Messiah?"

My reply came as gently as I could make it. "You see, the early Christians all *were* Jews, because that is exactly what did happen: *some* Jews who read their Torah carefully and believed and waited for the Messiah, *did* recognize and accept him as the one who fulfilled the prophecies. You see, Christianity *is* Jewish."

On the curve of a beautiful Italian beach the waves washed the sand with regular rhythm, and the spray caught the sun's mid-morning rays. A tall, grey-haired, handsome orthopedic surgeon was standing looking out at the horizon where the next day he would be disappearing as the ocean liner in the distance was becoming a speck. The next day he would be traveling back to the hospital in Israel where he was the chief.

"Thank you for your kindness in examining Franky yesterday."

"Oh, that's all right. I have so many patients who had polio the same year as he did. I have a special interest in comparing his progress with the progress of the patients in my hospital."

The conversation turned to his years in Israel, the fact that although he was an atheist himself he had a question to ask

ONE

which he could find no answer for logically. "Why is it that the Indian Jews, in India and absorbed in that culture for so many centuries, returned to Israel at such tremendous cost, such an upheaval to their lives, all because they heard that the land of Moses was being once more a nation of Jews? Why? It doesn't make sense ... unless ... unless ... but, you see, I don't believe there is a God."

"You're going tomorrow, and perhaps there won't be another time for conversation. I'd like to tell you what I think is the answer to that question."

It was 1963, but my answer to this Israeli surgeon was the same one as to the dentist, and the news editor—it was the bird's-eye view of the Bible.

A curly-headed little tot in bed asleep ... the father's agonized question based on his own unhappy experiences of childhood ... "Why oh why does he have to be a Jew?" An old dentist's question after years of contact with people wearing the label "Christian," "Why hasn't someone told me this before?" A Jewish 20th century student asking, "Why then haven't the Jews accepted this person as the one described by Isaiah as the Messiah?" A dignified, brilliant orthopedic surgeon, having come to Israel from Poland many years before, asking for an answer to a seemingly unanswerable question, "Why would Jews remain Jews in an alien culture for centuries and make the effort and sacrifice of going to an unknown land because of some remote tale handed down?" Why? Why? Why?

Why have the Gentile branches not understood the Olive tree into which they have been grafted, and why have they not been careful about the other branches among whom they bud and flower? And why have they not cared gently for the branches needing to be grafted back in? Why have the wild branches grafted in, not been longing to share the tree with the original branches? Why? Why? Why?

> *How odd of God*   *As those who choose*
> *To choose the Jew,*   *The Jewish God*
> *But not so odd*   *And hate the Jew.*

TWO

My husband often says there are only two possible beginnings to the universe. He says the third one would be "nothing nothing" to start with, which boggles the human mind too much to accept.

He puts it like this: "Either the universe had a personal beginning, or an impersonal beginning. The universe is therefore either an impersonal universe, or a personal one. If it is an impersonal universe, the evolvement of personality is a sad thing, because there is no satisfactory explanation giving meaning to thinking, acting, communicating, loving, having ideas, choosing, being full of creativity, and responding to the creativity of others. It is like a fish developing lungs in an airless universe. The longings and aspirations of personality drown without fulfillment."

The "impersonal beginning of all things" was spun out to me eloquently with poetic choice of words, dramatic tone of voice, and a certainty of the assurance that this *was* the way it all happened. It was not a university but a group of leaders being spoken to, and I was a little person sitting near the back of a filled auditorium. The speaker was a well qualified scientist, a Nobel prize winner, an intellectual of the twentieth century, a fascinating personality, and a Jew. This was a Jew who had long since discarded Genesis as far as history goes, and who therefore had but one choice left, the impersonal beginning of all things.

With depth of feeling in his voice which brought intentness to listening ears he began: "Billions and billions of years ago, eons and eons of time ago, there was nothing but particles moving about in chaotic disorder. And *suddenly—by chance—*two came together with an affinity for each other." He went on to spin out a succession of formulas, each of which had a chance beginning. I was astonished to hear in the condensed time of one hour, the unfolding of a faith accepting that *time* plus *chance* were the only two factors involved in all that we taste, see, feel, think about, observe emotionally, intellectually or psychologically, or discover through years of study. As the hour went on, this man with his honest assurance of this explanation being correct, said, "Four hundred years ago a collection of molecules wrote Hamlet." Musicians were spoken about, such as Beethoven and others, and finally a plea was being made concerning the ridding of the world of the stockpile of atomic weapons, and a warning was given that we must be careful not to let the destruction of the algae in the sea continue, or we would soon be without enough oxygen to survive. At the end a plea was made very passionately in the words of another Jew centuries ago, a Jew who was living on another base entirely. The speaker said, "I have no place for the supernatural in my scheme of things, but I am one who reads the Bible, and I want to quote from this book: 'Therefore choose life, that you and your descendants may live.' "

Ezekiel pled with the people of Israel as he prefaced his speaking with, "Thus saith the Lord,..." basing his life on another beginning entirely. Ezekiel was not begging men to keep the earth populated century after meaningless century, but telling them that God had a message for them that had to do with a different life altogether. "Cast away from you all your transgressions, whereby ye have transgressed; and make you a new heart and a new spirit: for why will ye die, O house of Israel? For I have no pleasure in the death of him that dieth, saith the Lord God: Wherefore turn yourselves, and live ye." Yes, turn to the Lord, and *live*, has a meaning quite beyond the possibility of even speaking such words as "choose" into an impersonal collection of molecules. How can a collection of

TWO

molecules chemically predetermined by its formula, choose anything? And how can there be a mixing up, a melange, of the words of a "myth" to give emotional impact in the midst of an impersonal universe? Something here doesn't "fit." The jigsaw puzzle is all askew.

If one chooses the impersonal beginning, one must go on to a logical conclusion of an impersonal universe, and an insignificant human being, and a meaningless history.

Before going on to the rest of the book which is to show the reality of what flows forth from the biblical explanation of all things, it is important to briefly mention what has taken place as man has gone on through years of trying, to find a philosophic explanation—springing from the impersonal beginning. Round and round the dark room, men have gone, trying to find truth, trying to find the "exit"—and they have concluded that there is "no exit." There is no truth, no need to look for it, it does not exist. Hegel, the German philosopher, came up with a new way of thinking. My husband has gone into this in detail in his books. Let me just say that one cannot understand the despair of modern man, nor as Isaiah wrote it, "Darkness shall cover the earth, and gross darkness the people" as a good description of that despair, one cannot understand without realizing some tiny fraction what it means to try to live on the basis of an impersonal beginning, plus Hegel's relativism.

Words, words, words? *Is* it just words? "It's like this," said Hegel, with the sudden excitement of an explorer. "Here is a thesis ..." and he must have put an imaginary dot in the air: • "And next to it is an antithesis ..." and now he had this: • • "It is all very simple; you come to a synthesis like so: •⋰• "Then you don't stop, but you take that *top* dot and call it a new thesis, •⋰ and another dot by it to make a new antithesis, and you get another synthesis." •⋰•⋰

"Gobbledegook," you say. "So what difference does that make to me?" Or perhaps you say, "*Sure,* everything is relative, so what? Everyone knows that."

But consider a minute that what is being said is that if you take right, and wrong, you come up with something that is a

19

mixture, and you go on with that to take a new step of
mixture. You take black and white and get grey, and take grey
to mix with another color to get something else. "So what?" Well,
so you come out with absolutely no base for morals, or
government, or law, because there is no *absolute,* there is no
way of having a *fixed* point for justice, or action, or teaching
your children. There is no right or wrong, there is no assurance
that the stove will not freeze tomorrow. All is in a state of flux,
and there is nothing which remains stable to give you a
continuity. You have no basis for judgment or for life.

Mix together in a bowl: an impersonal beginning which brings
you to a place of being a chance collection of molecules in a
chance universe, with the consideration that everything you
think, feel, or know is only *relative,* and you come out with man
living, as my husband calls it, "Under the line of despair." The
gross blackness that man lives in is that not only is there no
God, but he himself is no longer the significant person in
history which man has considered himself to be through
centuries. Even the blackness does not have a solid wall. If
everything is relative, really so, then the round room has oozy,
icky, soft walls which are not even a solid barrier in the
search for a door. Gross darkness covers the earth, and the
people of the earth. That verse in Isaiah 60 goes on to say that
the Lord shall arise upon people, and his glory shall be seen.
You've heard it sung perhaps, "Arise, shine, for thy light is
come." Again in verse 20 we are told, "Thy sun shall no more
go down, neither shall thy moon withdraw itself: for the Lord shall
be thine everlasting light, and the days of thy mourning shall be
ended." Yes, the Old Testament Isaiah is speaking to Israel.
Happily it can also apply to the other people of the earth, the
Gentiles. There *is* Someone at home in the universe. There is
Someone to look up to. There is a light in the darkness. There
is a door in the wall. There is *truth* to be found. There is
another possibility of another kind of a beginning. Beginning
at this other beginning, there is another end!

Do we *have* to be under the line of despair, and in all logical
thinking, all logical research, all logical feeling, come out to
the answer that man is a machine, a bundle of nervous reflexes,

TWO

a collection of chemical reactions, a predetermined creature
because of the chance arrangement of the molecules grinding
on to a new chance arrangement? Do we *have* to take a "leap
of faith" because we can't stand to be where our intellect says
we have to be ... and in this illogical, unexplained, nonsensical,
unreasonable *leap*, leap up away from the place of despair into
a drug experience, a mystical religious experience, an occult
experience of some sort, an escape in any kind of form? Do we
have to find some kind of a crutch ... quoting quotes which have
no meaning, but which are like a drug to our quivering senses,
like an aspirin pill for our searingly painful logic, like a
mystical meaningless poetry, but which give us a momentary
relief? It is all we are offered *if* we begin with the beginning of
impersonal particles or energy. It is all we are offered if we
begin with *no* absolute ... no *person* ... no personality there
to think or act or feel or choose or create or love or
communicate.

And what is the personal beginning?

What follows a personal beginning?

What is the logical conclusion of a personal beginning?

What are the answers to ... who am I? What is my purpose for
existing? What is ahead of me? Is there any life after death?
What possible base is there for moral judgments? Does
history have any meaning? Is my place in history significant at
all? What *are* the answers if one starts with a personal beginning?

Thinking back to our evening of sitting by a fire in the Bear
Mountain Lodge talking to a Jewish writer, thinking back to
my evening sitting on the bottom step of the Saint Louis
dentist's home, thinking back to the Sunday afternoon talking to
the news editor in that Swiss Alpine Chalet, thinking back to
the conversation at the edge of the Mediterranean Sea
talking to the Israeli surgeon—what *was* "the bird's-eye view of
the Bible" that brought forth an amazed reaction such as, "Isn't
this a *Jewish* religion?"?

THREE

It is necessary to start with the first book of Moses. "In the beginning God." That is to say, in the beginning a Person—an Infinite Person, but truly a person. In the beginning thinking, acting, feeling, love, communication, ideas, choice, creativity. Yes, in the beginning this God who made man in His image. Personality already existing. A personal universe created by a Person. A "people-oriented universe" created by a Person. A universe with fulfillment in it for the aspirations of artists, poets, musicians, landscape gardeners, because it has been created by an Artist, Poet, Musician, Landscape Gardener. Man made in the image of One who is a Creator ... so that man is made to be creative. Bach, Beethoven, Tolstoy, Leonardo di Vinci ... not accidental arrangements of molecules by chance creating, but men made in the image of God who are *amazing* because they are men with capabilities of both appreciating what other people create, and of creating themselves, in a variety of areas. Compassion not suddenly appearing out of nowhere, but compassion already there in the One who made man in His image.

Jessica's question comes, "Mummy, who made this house?" "Mummy, who made that statue?" "Mummy, who made TV in the first place?" And the answer is, "A person."

"An architect thought up this house in his mind, and then chose what he would do.

"The architect had a name, Mr. Kundig. He had lots of ideas

in his mind. Nobody could see those ideas until he chose to put them on paper and then chose one plan for this house. Then Mr. Kundig chose a plumber, Mr. Richard, and showed him where the bathroom was to be, and the kitchen, and the furnace. Mr. Richard had ideas, chose some of them, put them on paper ... and then the two men chose together exactly what kind of a bathroom and kitchen to make. Dear little Jessica, we'll have to have a long talk someday about who made this house, because there were electricians like Mr. Anex, and painters like Mr. Adler, and there were men who made and then put in the rugs, and made the roof, and others who made the furniture like Mr. Orting and curtains like Mr. Fretz. Oh, yes, all of this house, many parts of it were *inside those men's* heads, in their minds, before we could see, or live in it."

"The statue? Well, that statue was in your father's head, because he is a sculptor. Then he took clay and made it. Here is a picture of a statue Michaelangelo chipped out of marble, but it was first in his mind too; now you can see it. Yes, the TV was in a boy's head once—a boy of fourteen years old, who wrote a long formula on the blackboard in his school showing his ideas, before it was made. *Everything* was in someone's mind first of all. Everything that you see was first an idea, then someone chose to make it rather than something else. Come on now, let's have supper ... and you can taste as well as see what Mummy had in her head when she planned supper."

And who made the stars? Who made the mountains of Switzerland, India, and Canada? Who made the seas and the fantastic variety of fish within them? Who made the sunsets and the glorious songs of the birds? Who made an orderly universe, so precise that men can calculate with preciseness and go to the moon?

Does the "test tube" which is me, you, not tell us that all things were *made* first in the realm of ideas, and then by choice into the seen world to communicate something of the maker to other people?

If you discard the possibility of the existence of the architect, the plumber, the electrician, the scientist, the cook, the gardener ... *another* answer must be given to the children's

THREE

questions. There is no need searching for the name of these persons, nor indeed for the persons, if no person is there.

But if you come to realize that the universe must have had a personal beginning, that it really is a people universe, you breathe a sigh of great relief when you discover that a verbalizing God, able to communicate with the verbalizing people He created, has put into understandable words the account we need to know concerning the beginning.

Moses was given by inspiration the understanding and factual knowledge to impart in words to those who would follow, as he told what God told him, "In the beginning God." In the book of Job God speaks, asking, "Where wast thou when I laid the foundations of the earth? declare it if thou hast understanding ... Knowest thou it because thou wast then born? Or because the number of thy days is so great?... Shall he that contendeth with the Almighty instruct him? he that reproveth God, let him answer it."

The Psalmist in Psalm 104 sings with awe of the creative ability of God, "who maketh the clouds his chariot: who walketh upon the wings of the wind:... who laid the foundations of the earth, that it should not be removed forever.... He watereth the hills from his chambers: the earth is satisfied with the fruit of thy works." Isaiah makes plain the danger of man's accepting another answer as he says, "And forgettest the Lord thy maker, that hath stretched forth the heavens, and laid the foundations of the earth? ... but I am the Lord thy God, that divided the sea, whose waves roared, the Lord of hosts is his *name*." In another place Isaiah tells the people, and us, "Thus saith God the Lord, he that created the heavens, and stretched them out: he that spread forth the earth, and that which cometh out of it; he that giveth breath unto the people upon it, and spirit to them that walk therein: I the Lord have called thee ... I am the Lord: that is my *name*...." And again Isaiah speaks to the Jews of that time who were turning to other answers, and whom he was calling back in God's words to them, and to us, "But now saith the Lord that created thee, O Jacob, and he that formed thee, O Israel, Fear not: for I have redeemed thee, I have called thee by thy name; thou art mine."

Again Isaiah, "I am the Lord, your Holy One, the creator of Israel, your King. Thus saith the Lord, which maketh a way in the sea and a path in the mighty waters."

There was a personal beginning. There was a person there to have ideas. There were three persons to love, communicate, choose, and create. The LORD we are told, is His *name*. And He did not leave us without a verbalized condensation of the history we needed to know to understand something of the situation in which we are now. He has given us enough to explain the order of the universe, the preciseness of the movement of the planets, but also enough to understand something of who we are, and whether life is worth living, and what He promises is ahead. Are we only a collection of molecules foolishly agonizing for survival ... or is the *life* we are urged to choose described by Isaiah when he said, "Since the beginning of the world men have not heard, nor perceived by the ear, neither hath eye seen, O God, beside thee, what he hath prepared for him that waiteth for him."

Is it true that we cannot imagine the wonders of the *unspoiled* beauty ahead being prepared for us to see, hear, feel, taste, smell? Can we see enough of the leftover beauty of God's creation to have an excitement about seeing it restored?

Have you ever been through an art museum after it was vandalized? Have you ever seen a beautiful home after vandals got through with it? Have you come back to a place you yourself made beautiful—a garden, an art work, a room you had put together with a perfectionist's taste—right after violent, senseless vandals had slashed it up? Perhaps then you have a very small understanding of the necessity to explain to people in words something of what you expect to do as you restore the devastating destruction, and as you promise to them that they will be amazed when they see it. You cannot explain this to your dog, or your goldfish—but you can to your child. "Honey, wait till you see how it will all be when Daddy and Mummy fix it all up. Your doll house will be better than before, and we'll plant another garden with a greater variety of plants than we had in the other one." Perhaps you have restored paintings, maybe that is your profession. Perhaps you

THREE

have restored old furniture, ruined by people who don't appreciate antiques. Maybe then you have the background, having been made as a person in the image of a Person, to begin to have some understanding of destruction of what has been made, and the need of a solution so that there may be a restoration. Just any old solution wouldn't fit.

Destruction? Vandals? What is being driven at? Yes, the first book of Moses tells us that we are to understand, we verbalizing creatures whom God has made in His image, who then also can verbalize, the exact history of what happened. We are not being told myths as if we had no intelligence to understand the realities of what took place, but we are meant to be able to *know* and understand—we who have *names*, Deborah, Etian, Joseph, John, Mary, Priscilla, Gennie, Daniel, Abraham, Sarah, Susan, Abbigail, Naomi, Samuel, David—we are meant to understand what a Person with a *name* has put into words. We have not been given a poetic aspirin pill with which to jump out of reality into fantasy, but we have been given history and the intelligence to listen to that history and understand our present dilemma.

So Moses writes what God gave him knowledge to write as he tells us that all things were made good, and that man made in God's image had a place of dominion over the fish of the sea, the birds of the air, and the animals of the earth. Adam, being finite, had a place of loneliness, because although he was a person, in communication with God who also was personal, still Adam was finite, and God was infinite. So we are told God said that it is not good for man to be alone, and God made a helpmate for him. God made another finite person so that communication could take place horizontally as well as vertically. God made a person who could relate to that first person on a finite level in every way. We are told that God took a rib from Adam after putting him into a deep sleep (as in an operating room one is put to sleep in some way), and out of this rib He made a woman. *If* there is a Personal Infinite Eternal God, is it a problem to think of Him creating things in a variety of ways? Is it a problem to imagine God creating a fantastically beautiful woman out of the cells contained in a rib, when you

see your own baby come forth nine months after having
been just two miniscule cells—now perfect with eyes, ears,
feet, fingers, a voice with which to cry—all in nine months time?
If God is truly Creator, His making of Adam as a separate
creation to be in the image of a Person, and His making Eve
from the rib of Adam, is no problem at all. The basic problem is
"which beginning?" It is a greater problem to think of having faith
to believe in *order* coming out of *chaos*, by *chance*. We have no
example to see, no test tube where it is being done today.

So Adam and Eve are given the marvelous garden,
landscaped for them by the Gardener who also created the plants
in the first place, and who comes to talk with them evening
after cool evening, at the end of perfect day after perfect
day: the garden of Eden. Paradise that was to be lost.

But what happened to ruin it? Where did the vandal come
from?

We need to go back a bit. It is Isaiah who has been given
by God a piece of the jigsaw puzzle of history to fit in for us to
know where sin originated. Before God created human beings,
He had already created angels. What do we know about
angels? Not everything certainly, but something. They are
rational creatures with choice, not programmed computers.
They had a length of existence in the created universe, before
man was created, but how long their period of choice was, we
are not told. God, who is a God of diversity as well as of
unity, created snowflakes so that no two are exactly alike. God
is able to create trees with no two leaves on any one tree exactly
alike. There is tremendous unity in the original ecological
balances in the world, but tremendous variety in all of
created nature. I often think of the beauty of handmade fabric,
the wonder of handmade pottery, the loveliness of handmade
embroidery, the specialness of art never to be exactly copied
by any hands other than the ones that made the original.
Machines can make things all alike. The description of Lucifer,
the highest of angels, causes us to know that angels have names
and personalities that differ. Lucifer was the most beautiful of
the angels, called son of the morning, but during the period
of choice, he chose to rebel against the leadership of God. He

THREE

chose to be equal with God, and also to have a throne that other angels might worship him. The rebellion became the conflict of the ages. This was the conflict which brought sin into the universe. This was the war of the created being against the Creator. Isaiah in chapter 14:12 to 17 briefly tells us that one day Lucifer, who was thrown out of the heavens along with the angels who joined him (who became demons), will be cast down, defeated completely, and that people at that time will look at him with amazement saying, "Could this possibly be the one who caused all the disruption in the earth, who brought about all the horrible things which shook the kingdoms of the world, who vandalized the world into a wilderness, and who caused cities to be destroyed?"

Yes, this is the vandal who caused the world to become a spoiled place. The vandal who stalked through God's art museum with a hatred which slashed out in meaningless destruction. This is the vandal who was the forerunner of Hitler and Goering, who with the same type of bitterness resolved that even if he was going to lose the war, he would take as much "down" with him as possible—that nothing would be left, or as little as possible, for his enemy, God.

Evil is not an impersonal bowl of something that spilled out into the world. Evil is a matter of choice, and that choice has to take place in a rational mind. Sin is first in the realm of the mind, and then takes place in actions. There is a tremendous choice involved in Lucifer's saying, "I *will* exalt my throne above the stars of God: I *will* ascend into heaven ... I *will* be like the most High...." The plan to lead an aggressive attack against the Triune God and the faithful loyal angels, was the first battle plan, the first war. This war still continues, and all other wars have some relationship to it. It is not an impersonal chance happening that this angel revolted and drew others into the revolt; it is an act of the will. Personality is involved in the act of one's will. Computers have no will of their own. Puppets have no will with which to act.

The reality of a personal universe is seen not only in the creation we observe, feel, taste, hear, but in the constant evidence within us of this struggle: "To do or not to do, that is the question." We have a choice to make moment by moment, we *know* we have choice. We can be told we are a chance collection of molecules making us into machines, but our experience cuts across this, and people crash their heads into the reality of the choices affecting their own lives, the choices they even deny exist: to do or not to do.

How does Satan, Lucifer, the leader of the fallen angels, affect the world? How does he succeed in causing the perfection of creation to be spoiled?

FOUR

After God's creation of Adam and Eve, and His constant communication with them and relationship with them day by day, how long was it before Lucifer, now Satan, waited to make his attack? We have no record of the length of time, but we are told that one day he came in the form of a serpent and spoke to Eve saying, "Hath God said, Ye shall not eat of every tree of the garden?" A subtle injection of doubt in Eve's mind. The implication was that perhaps God had not spoken the truth. Eve knew God had told them to eat of every tree except one. Eve answered that God had told them that if they ate of the fruit of that one particular tree they would die. However, one feels the seed of doubt in her mind even as she speaks these words.

Satan is not very original. His subtle question is really the same through the centuries, and in this century. Every human being who has ever heard or read the words in the Bible hears Satan's question at one time or another: "Hath God said this? Is this really the Word of God? Can you trust this as being truth? Or—?" He implants the doubt that is the forerunner of denial that God's communication to man is true truth.

Satan's flat contradiction of God's word to Adam and Eve came next as he said dogmatically, "Ye shall not surely die." In other words Satan is saying God has lied. The serpent continues, "God knows that in the day you eat this fruit, you shall be as gods, knowing good and evil." God is trying to keep you ignorant.

If only you eat you will be brilliant and wise with instant knowledge.

Here are two totally contradictory statements. One is true. One is false. Here is a most important demonstration of the reality of choice. The choice involved is one of choosing to believe that one statement is true, and one is false. It is a matter of believing God or Satan. This is not a mystical airy-fairy kind of "faith," but a conviction that is needed, a trust, a faith, that one or the other was speaking true truth, and then *acting* on that faith, belief, trust, conviction. If Eve and Adam believe that God has spoken the truth, and choose to act upon that, neither one of them would eat the fruit of that one tree. They would not choose to die. This is not suicide. Their choice to eat is on the basis that they believe Satan has spoken the truth when he said they would gain knowledge and wisdom. They eat believing. They eat with faith. But their faith is in the wrong person. Faith in itself is not any special thing. It is the *person* that is trustworthy who makes faith of value. Belief that Satan has spoken the truth is shown in an action which demonstrated clearly that Eve and then Adam were convinced that God had *not* spoken the truth.

If they had loved God, they would have wanted to please Him, so it was an act of unlove. If they had been eager to obey God they would not have gone contrary to His command. If they had believed God they would not have believed the lie of Satan. And one more thing: if they had niggling doubts arise in their minds, they *could* have said, "We'll ask in our talk together tonight with God, as we walk in the cool of the evening, and He will *explain* to us who you are and why you have presented this diametrically opposed statement to us." Because you see, they had an open communication with God.

But they rushed ahead to eat, believing Satan rather than God, and plunging themselves, and the generations to follow them, into darkness. Death has now entered the universe. Death is separation. Adam and Eve are separated from communication with God, and they have to leave the garden. Adam and Eve's perfect relationship with each other is spoiled, and separation

FOUR

of person from person begins. Separation psychologically of the person inside had its beginning. Separation of body and soul was ahead, but disease and physical pain and brokenness began. The universe became abnormal. Satan had walked through God's "art museum"—that is, the art work of God's hands—and had vandalized it with slashes of senseless destruction, trying to separate people from God, and in his declared battle he planned to continue this drive to separate people from God, with seemingly endless lies to contradict true truth in a variety of ways. Satan and his followers were to have a certain length of time before the end of this rebellion would come. We are still in that period of time before the end.

Why choice in the first place? You may ask this with thoughts of everything being good. Can you imagine a computer loving, feeling, appreciating music, having abstract thoughts, communicating ideas? God did not make people as little machine models of Himself when He made man in His own image. God made people in His image as personalities who could think, act, feel, have ideas, choose, communicate, create. Choice is involved in whether to speak or to keep quiet, whether to say everything that it is possible to say, or to select what would be helpful or relevant to a situation. Choice is involved in loving a person and asking that one to marry. Choice is involved in every kind of creativity. Choice is involved in every moment of life, mundane or fantastic—whether to go to a concert, or to dig manure in a garden instead of commercial fertilizer. God did not make programmed computers, or mechanized dolls such as children play with. "I want a *real* baby," is often the plea of a five-year-old envious of a cousin's baby sister. The dolls do not suffice to substitute for real personality even in its tiniest, youngest form. A human being made in the image of God is different, from the moment of birth.

Choice gives significance in a significant history. In other words, a person's choice gives that person an amount of dignity. One may say, "Slaves are in a good position, they have all they need to eat, a place to sleep, no worries of choice." Or, "Prisoners have no pressures, they are told what to do." The dignity involved in having choice to do or not to do, is a dignity every human being was meant to have. "Choice" is not the matter of being given a bowl of evil spilling drops into the world, and a bowl of good likewise filled. "Choice" is the basis of all rational thinking and acting, of all communication and creativity which communicates something that was in the person's mind, of all love in every form. Choice is a basic ingredient of freedom. Choice is a basic ingredient of purpose. Choice is a basic ingredient of incentive. Choice is basic in relationships ... the vertical relationship of human beings with God, and the horizontal relationships of human being with human being.

If you are tempted to wipe out choice by drugging the world into chemically controlled actions, remember you are wiping out one of the basic ingredients of man, woman, people, human beings created in the image of God.

So Adam and Eve's very real historic period of time in close relationship with God in a perfect environment, came to an end on the basis of their choice, so real and so significant that history was changed. Eve, in making the first choice, was not considered unimportant because she was a woman. Her choice was so significant that it brought about titanic historic results. God treated woman and man with fairness, and as important in the history of the universe.

Was that the end of any possible communication with God? Did that end any possible relationship with God? Had Satan succeeded in cutting off people from God forever? Could the Trinity think of *any* way of restoring the situation, of defeating the purpose of Satan? Had Satan shown that he was stronger than God in causing people to believe his lies then, and century after century from that time on?

Before God told Eve and Adam the sad facts of cause and effect, of the sequence of results following choice, of the fact that justice on the part of a Holy God means fulfilling the warning before given, "If you eat, death will follow"—Before God explained all that the results would mean in the world now to be abnormal, now to be changed from its perfect state to its spoiled state—God *first* gave the one possible solution the

FOUR

Trinity had decided upon for a future restoration, for a final victory over what Satan had done.

God spoke directly to Satan—Lucifer the rebellious fallen angel, Lucifer the destructive one who would be inspiring the "Hitlers" of history. God said to Satan, "I will put enmity between thee and the woman, and between thy seed and her seed; it shall bruise thy head, and thou shalt bruise his heel." There is going to be a conflict between you, Satan, and the woman, and one day someone is going to be born of a woman—someone who will come as the seed of a woman—who will have victory over you, even though you will give him a wound. This is the *first* promise of the Messiah, and it is made *first*, even before the details of the "curse" are unfolded. There is no lapse of time between the fall of the human race, and the promise that there will be a victory over what has happened, a restoration of the destruction. Eve and Adam are given hope immediately, and are given another statement by God to *believe*. They are trusted with an area in which to demonstrate their belief of a promise. Yes, the promise is for something in the future, but the demonstration of their belief that God has spoken truth is something possible to them in *their* moment of history.

So as Adam and Eve listen to the facts being unfolded that cause and effect are going to be experienced, as they listen to the list of things which will give them some inkling of the changes to come, already they have ringing in their ears the verbalized statement of *hope* ... hope in a coming solution. Yes, conception is to be multiplied and babies will not now be perfectly spaced. Yes, there will be pain in childbirth, and sweat upon the brow as hard work will be needed to bring forth the food to feed wife and children. Yes, there will be thorns, thirst, sickness, and signs of death in all that will surround them. *But* if they *believe* what God has said, there is hope, hope singing through with a music that eases the pain. Hope that promises, "This isn't the end; there is something ahead. Things can be put back together again someday. We need now really to *believe God*, and act upon this belief."

The Holy God, the perfectly Just God, has acted upon the basis of His perfect holiness and perfect justice to bring results—the promised results after the choice of His created people was made to rebel against Him and to believe that He had lied—and to act upon that belief. But the Loving God, the Compassionate God, had already given an embryo promise which was to be constantly more clear as history moved along, a promise which could from the first moment it was given be *believed.*

Did Adam and Eve believe? We are not told. We are told of God's clothing them with a fur covering, the skin of an animal which had to die to cover their nakedness. Why weren't the leaves they picked enough to make a covering? Because they needed another step of explanation to make their understanding more vivid. An animal had to die to cover their nakedness which was a result of the rebellious choice they had made. They had needed no covering at all until they sinned. They had not known shame in any slight degree. Now shame floods over them and they grab for a covering as a way of hiding from the eyes of God. Oh, sinful Eve, oh, sinful Adam, this work of your hands isn't enough to cover the awfulness of what you have done. The covering of your sin is only going to be possible if a terrible price is paid. At the moment, this animal must suffer the death your action (based on your belief that Satan was speaking truth and God a lie) has brought into the universe. You now have before your eyes, Adam and Eve, a demonstration of what sudden death—death so that you might be covered—is like.

Do you think they would have forgotten that powerful illustration? Do you think as their hands smoothed the softness of the skin clothing, they would have forgotten their first glimpse of violent death, and *something* of the understanding that it was because of their sin?

We cannot know what went on in the minds and understanding of Adam and Eve, but God has not left to our imagination what came next in His unfolding to the human race the way back to communication with Himself.

Cain and Abel, as sons of Adam and Eve, surely had some explanation of what had happened in the past lives of their

FOUR

parents. We know they knew of God's existence because they came to make "an offering unto the Lord." It was not a problem to them as to whether God existed or not, they both brought an offering. In some way it had been explained to them what kind of offering to bring. From all the rest of the Bible we know that God has told parents to teach their children the truth about Himself, and about how to come to Him. It would not be according to the character of God to suppose these two boys had not been told as much as Adam and Eve knew about the promise, and about how sin must be cared for as one is coming into God's presence.

Now we can imagine two altars. Perhaps they were of rough, unpolished stone. Cain brings his fruits and vegetables, a beautiful array—perhaps an artistic arrangement with oranges, polished applies, artichokes, bananas, cabbages, bright carrots, shining purple onions, green grapes trailing their curls and leaves over the edges of the stone. "How spiritual!" one might exclaim. One might think of a variety of outwardly beautiful offerings one could make, the work of one's hands, the creativity of one's imagination which would match the beauty of this offering. Abel brings a little lamb, a perfect one —a "firstling of the flock"—and kills it to place on the altar. How unbeautiful! What a sight to turn away from. What has this to do with worship?

We are told that God accepted Abel's offering. Abel was really accepted into the presence of God. Why? On the basis of the lamb. God rejected Cain's offering, making Cain angry indeed. Why rejected? Because Cain came with his own works, the result of his *defiance* of what God had said. Cain came *not* believing that he had to come in any special way, refusing to come in any special way. Cain came saying, in essence, "You can just accept me, God, as I do my own thing. I'm not going to believe it is necessary to do anything other than my *own thing*."

In the book of Hebrews in the New Testament, written to Jews to make things clear to them at that time, chapter eleven verse four says, "By faith Abel offered unto God a more excellent sacrifice than Cain, by which he obtained certainty that he was

37

righteous,..." What is this saying? It is saying that because Abel *believed* what God had said, because he had faith in the truth of God's given way of coming to Himself being necessary, because he chose to come with a sin offering which was the one God had said was needed, he was therefore accepted by God. The verse goes on to say that although Abel is dead (and as Cain killed him in anger, he died very early) he "yet speaketh." That is to say, Abel died young, but the fact of his believing God is still "speaking" to people. Abel's belief is still a help to other people in making clear to them what God wants them to know. Abel's action demonstrated his inward belief in what God had said, to anyone who cared to look—to angels, to Lucifer if he were lurking around, to his brother who did not appreciate it, to God, and to any who would hear the story of what he did at any point in history. Also God's acceptance of Abel's sacrifice made it clear to anyone (other brothers and sisters, Adam and Eve themselves—all who would hear the story down through the years) that coming with the lamb was really the way to come to God, looking forward in belief to a fulfillment of a promise that one day someone was coming who would fulfill the promise already given.

If it had been possible for us to stand there that day looking out over the future of history springing forth from those two altars, we might have seen something like this, if centuries could be charted into a kind of graph. Simply two lines—but what a profound truth these two lines can illustrate! People, mankind, human beings divided into two kinds—not black and white, not rich and poor, not educated and uneducated—simply those who have believed God, believed what He has said, believed His word and have acted upon that belief; and those who have *not* believed Him, but who have said in one form or another "I'll do my *own thing*." All religions that have ever been thought up by man have had something in common, and that is that they think that through works, religious works or moral works, they will be accepted by whatever concept of God they have, or by what they might call their spiritual universe.

From the moment Adam and Eve turned to believe Satan,

FOUR

and God spoke to them about the results, there has been only one way to come back into communication and relationship with the true living God who created all things.

Cain and Abel's sacrifices demonstrated this in a way that all who followed could have been aware.

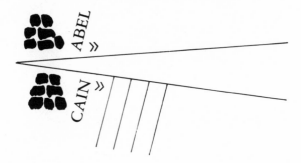

Abel's bringing of the lamb was with *some* measure of understanding that he himself could not make up for what had been done, that it was impossible to figure out a way of paying for sin oneself, that it was necessary for the price to be paid in another way, and that God had really spoken truth when He said to come with the lamb, as a sacrifice.

We need to hurry along as we take a bird's-eye view of the Bible so that you can have a grasp of the continuity through history.

FIVE

Was Abel a Jew, and was Cain a Gentile? No, of course not. There were two streams of people, but not yet had the people of God been given a specific and more detailed "covenant." Abel was dead, but Adam and Eve had other children who believed God, and Cain went off to another geographical location with his wife, to form a branch of civilization elsewhere.

We know that at the time of Noah there were no people, outside of his family, left who believed God; the majority had rebelled and believed a lie rather than the truth. Noah was given a definite message from God to give the people, but they simply laughed at him, and in scorn declared that this message was not true. They were asked to believe that the word, the verbalized message of God, was true, just the same as Eve and Adam had been given a true statement to believe or not believe. Not only was Noah worshiping in the correct way with the right sacrifice demonstrating that he believed God, but when God told him to prepare an ark for the coming flood, he believed and acted upon that belief in the midst of a jeering crowd! The ark was open for a long time for any who would join Noah and his family before the flood came, but no one came to join them! The minority who did believe were safe in the ark while the earth was being destroyed, but others could have been inside if they had acted on the basis of God's warning message being true truth.

In the book of Hebrews we are told that "by faith Noah, being warned of God of things not seen yet, moved with fear (born of belief that the flood was really going to come), prepared an ark to the saving of his family; by which he condemned the world, and became an heir of righteousness which is by faith." The writer of Hebrews is saying to Jews here that Noah inherited the same "righteousness" that later Abraham was going to be given because of his belief and faith in the truth of God's statements. Noah, in other words, was not only saved from the flood because of his belief in God, but he had come to God in the right way, and followed along in the line of Abel, looking ahead to the fulfillment of the promises. Noah had sufficient knowledge to come to God even as Abel had come. But Noah preached to others, so it was not merely a matter of knowledge, but of believing God and then acting accordingly.

Now Abraham lived in Ur of the Chaldees where it is said that people worshiped the moon goddess, and their culture was highly developed. Square root was taught there, as well as moon-shaped cakes being made to commemorate the false worship. One must not think that uneducated people lived in the city Abraham left.

Yes, Abraham was told by the Lord to get out of this country, leaving family as well as friends, and to go to a land that God would show him. A very great promise was made to Abraham, this man who believed God, as he was told by the Eternal One, "I will make of thee a great nation, and I will bless thee, and make thy name great and thou shalt be a blessing. And I will bless them that bless thee, and curse him that curseth thee: and in thee shall all the families of the earth be blessed."

This tremendous promise seems to fit in with the promise made to Adam and Eve. It seems to say that the time has come when God has chosen a man to head the family from which one day the person will be born who will bring the looked for "solution" or victory. It becomes exciting to follow the story and see what happened next. We are told in Hebrews, written especially for the Jews, that Abraham went out by faith, when he was called to go out into a place which he should afterwards receive for an inheritance—and that he obeyed and

FIVE

went out not knowing whither he went. His belief in God's word
to him was tremendous. Not only did he go out into fields and
hills, far away from his accustomed comforts and way of life,
but when God spoke to him saying that Sarah would have a
child in her old age, he believed that God was able to do what
seemed impossible. In the book of Hebrews we are told that
Sarah, too, judged God to be really One who would be
faithful to His own promises, that what He said He would do,
He *would* do! Sarah believed God could do this miracle in her
body, and that she could conceive in her old age.

So we are told that from these two people too old to have
children, there "sprang forth so many as the stars of the sky in
multitude and as the sand which is by the sea shore innumerable."
It was a picture of *life* coming forth abundantly from those
who, humanly speaking, were already dead, *not* of the age to
have children. Furthermore we are told that Abraham looked
forward to the future with assurance, as "he looked for a city
which hath foundations, whose builder and maker is God."
Abraham was looking forward to the future city we are still
looking for. Abraham really believed; he believed what God
said to him about the present and about the future. As Jews all
look back to their forefather, the first Israelite, they look back
to one who believed God, and "it was counted to him for
righteousness."

How did Abraham worship? With the lamb as a sacrifice,
looking forward with some understanding to a coming person,
who, he has been told, will bless the peoples of the earth,
and now he knows this one will come from his descendants. As
his son Isaac is born, you can imagine with what love and special
excitement Abraham regards this son. Here is the one
promised by God, now in his arms. He might have felt that
this one would be the special blessing, as it was not known to
him how long a time it would be before the special one would
come. At any rate Abraham's whole trust in God's promise that
there would come forth a nation from his children and
grandchildren, pointed to the fact that Abraham expected
Isaac to have sons, and the grandsons to again have sons. Isaac was
a precious son in whom all the promises were really tied up.

Now we come to the day described in Genesis chapter twenty-two. God has called Abraham to come and offer Isaac his only son on one of the mountains in the land of Moriah. "I will point out which mountain," God says.

Abraham, trusting God with all his heart, believing the promises ahead of him will be fulfilled, starts out early in the morning with two servants, a load of wood for the burnt offering, and a saddled ass to help take them along the way. Isaac is with him. As this little party of men walk and ride along, a three-days' journey to the specific mountain where God was leading them, Abraham suddenly looks up and sees the place in the distance.

How do we know Abraham trusted God with all his heart? Because as he said to the young servants, "Wait here with the ass; the lad and I will go yonder and we will return to you." Abraham spoke in the plural, *"We* will return...." He shows confidence, knowing very well that God is not worshiped with human sacrifice, but with a lamb. Abraham knows the God whom he loves and trusts, and knows he can have confidence in Him. God has said Isaac will be the father of many people. Abraham then expects God either to prevent Isaac's death, or bring him back to life.

Abraham and Isaac walk up the mountain, Isaac carrying the wood, Abraham carrying fire and a knife. Knowing that a lamb is missing, Isaac speaks to his father, asking, "Where is the lamb for a burnt offering?" And Abraham's reply is, "God will provide himself a lamb for the burnt offering, my son." Isaac walks on, also showing confidence in God. Remember, Isaac is a young man, not a child; he is stronger than his old father and quite able to offer resistance. They walk on together, father and son, side by side, climbing with their burdens, trusting God together and trusting each other in their horizontal relationship.

Then they came to the place God had led them. It is a chosen spot, chosen by God for this particular moment in history, and for this particular happening—so important to them, and so important to the nation who would follow, and to all who are one day to be the spiritual seed of Abraham. An historic hill indeed.

FIVE

The fire, knife, and wood must have been put down, as an altar was built of stones, prepared for the sacrifice. As the wood is placed on the altar, unresistingly Isaac lets his father place him on the wood, bind him, and lift the knife—arm outstretched in a gesture, ready to let the knife fall.

Suddenly a voice comes out of heaven and says, "Abraham, Abraham," and Abraham replies, "Here am I." And the One in heaven says, "Lay not thine hand upon the lad, neither do him any harm: for now I know that thou fearest God, seeing thou hast not withheld thine only son from me."

Then Abraham looks up, and sees an amazing sight he had not seen before: a ram, the lamb needed for the sacrifice, is caught by his horns in a thicket, a tangle of bushes.

Has God been torturing Abraham and Isaac just to prove their love? No, it is much more than that. What is now about to take place is a very, *very* important demonstration to Abraham who is the father of the Jews, and to Isaac who is to be a leader of Israel, of just what the blessing that had been promised was all about. These two had to *understand* with their intellects as well as to believe that God was going to fulfill His promise that one day the nations of the earth would be blessed through their seed, their children and grandchildren down through generations. These two needed to teach children and grandchildren what God was going to make clear to them. Also the story needed to be recorded so that each generation could relive this moment with fresh understanding. The historic event that was to take place in a few moments was to picture a reality that would some day take place in the very middle of all history, so that every one who would believe could be taken off of the altar even as Isaac "escaped" that day. A substitution was to take place which would teach people what God's solution to the spoiled universe and to man's sin was all about. A substitution was to take place which would make the truth clear to those who needed to wait patiently for the future fulfillment, believing with a measure of understanding. This same substitution would also make the truth clear to those who would be looking *back* on history, as we are now.

Come to the hillside with Abraham and Isaac and become

involved in the understanding of that really dramatic moment. Isaac is loosed and stands free at the side of the altar. The ram is taken and substituted for Isaac. Abraham and Isaac looked at the dying ram taking Isaac's place. In our imaginations we can see the whole of the human race being offered a glimpse of this, being given the possibility of understanding, and we realize that the substitutionary atonement is being demonstrated and being pointed forward to with crystal-clear illustration that a child could understand.

The ram was dying in Isaac's place. This further step of understanding is being given to the already long history of lambs being the necessary sacrifice for entering into the presence of God. Isaac steps off, the ram is substituted. Will Isaac ever forget the feeling of that release? Will he ever be able to forget what it means to be free? Will Abraham ever forget the reality of the substitution when it was his only son involved? Don't you think father and son came to an understanding of the wonder of looking forward to the promised one, the Messiah who would come from their family and bless many people of all nations through something he would do? I am sure they would think back many many times, and discuss the future with fresh (vivid, real) expectation as they talked to each other and to their children and grandchildren of what took place that day.

For us, it is a vivid picture of what the Messiah would do, as He took the place of each one who comes to Him believing. You see, the God of detail—our God who is a perfectionist in caring for every tiny detail—gave Abraham a prophetic statement to give at the end of this titanic "incident." "Abraham called the name of the place Jehovah-jireh: as it is said to this day, In the mount of Lord it *shall* be seen."

What is the prophecy? It is that one day in the future there shall be seen in this mountain, in this geographic area, something very, *very* important. The word Jehovah-jireh means, "The Lord will provide." The Lord is going to provide the most essential provision of all for mankind in this mountain, in this area some day. And many years after that, in this very area, at Jerusalem, the Messiah would die, as a substitute. His death

FIVE

would not be the substitute for just *one* other *person,* as a human being's death would have to be. His death would not be for just *one time* of entering the presence of God on the part of other people, as the lamb's death had to be (time after time through the centuries of worship, time after time on the Day of Atonement as the Jews looked back to atonement as the blood of the lamb was sprinkled on the lid of the ark, the mercy seat). His death would be for *all* who would believe in Him as the Messiah, as the Lamb that had been pointed forward to for so long. "The Lord will provide," said Abraham. "In the mountain of the Lord it shall be seen in the future," said Abraham.

As Jews celebrated the Day of Atonement in ancient days, and then on through the years, they were meant to have *some* understanding of the substitutionary atonement of the Lamb, the Messiah, taking their place. We read in Leviticus, "And Aaron shall offer his bullock of the sin offering which is for himself and make an atonement for himself and for his household... And he shall take of the blood and sprinkle it with his finger on the mercy seat eastward ... and he shall make an atonement for the holy place, because of the uncleanness of the children of Israel, and because of all their transgressions in all their sins...." "For on that day shall the priest make an atonement for you, to cleanse you, that ye may be clean from all your sins before the Lord."

"And Moses said unto Aaron, Go unto the altar, and offer thy sin offering and thy burnt offering and make an atonement for thyself and for the people ... as the Lord commanded" (Leviticus 9:7).

Yes, Abraham understood something very clearly—not everything, but enough to look forward with faith, believing. Isaac understood something also very clearly, and shared with his father that wonderful moment as they together listened to Abraham's words ringing in their ears and in their faith-filled hearts, in their earnest expectation in belief. Both men, the young one and the old one, came down the mountainside that day rejoicing as they thought of the new name for the mountain ... "Jehovah-jireh." In the mount of the Lord it shall be seen ... the Lord will provide. They came

47

down to listen to the Lord with hearts bursting with trust and assurance that indeed the Lord was able to provide. They had just seen Him provide, and they knew He could do it in the future when the central moment would come in history—the moment when people could stop looking forward, and could look back at an event that had been finished, completed.

Abraham and Isaac came down that hill knowing they had been shown a substitution, and that they had been shown a place where the complete substitution would take place. They were ready to be given the special covenant God was going to make with them, first with Abraham as head of the entire family of Israel, then with Isaac, for as he listened he knew he would be next in line to carry on.

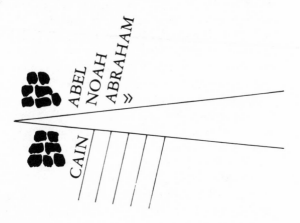

"In blessing I will bless thee, and in multiplying I will multiply thy seed as the stars of the heaven, and as the sand which is upon the seashore; and thy seed shall possess the gate of his enemies; and *in thy seed* shall *all* the *nations of the earth* be blessed; because thou hast obeyed my voice."

Many centuries after that, Peter, another Jew, one who had become convinced that the prophecies had been fulfilled, said in the book of the Acts to Jews: "Ye are the children of the prophets, and of the covenant which God made with our fathers, saying unto Abraham, And in thy seed shall all the

FIVE

kindreds of the earth be blessed. Unto you first God, having raised up his Son Jesus, sent him to bless you, in turning every one of you from his iniquities."

The seed of Abraham, born of a woman, opened the way to blessing to the Jew and to the non-Jew.

SIX

The atonement which had been demonstrated to Abraham and Isaac at the time of the substitution of the ram caught in the bushes, was celebrated and handed down to the next generation year after year, century after century, and, in a special way, from Moses' time on. But was that *all* there was in the unfolding of understanding to the growing family of Abraham, and to any others who cared to seek an *answer* in the midst of the abnormal universe?

Years passed by and the family of Abraham, through the seed of Isaac, increased. The twelve sons of Jacob were to be the fathers of twelve tribes, but as yet they were just brothers with particular jealousy and animosity against a younger brother, Joseph. Just briefly as we "fly with a bird" over this history, we need to stop to notice that as the brothers sold Joseph into slavery into Egypt, they meant it for harm to him, but we are later told that God turned it into good, not only for Joseph but also for the whole family.

Joseph believed God, and communicated with Him. As Joseph spent time in prison because of a false accusation, he became respected by the prison guard, and very much admired by the chief butler, whose dream Joseph had been able to correctly interpret. One day when Pharaoh had an unexplainable dream which bothered him, the butler remembered Joseph, and told of what he had done for him in prison. Pharaoh sent immediately for Joseph, who was shaved and prepared quickly for entrance before the ruler of the land, and commanded him to interpret his dream.

Joseph demonstrates his belief in God as he answers, "It is not in me: God shall give Pharaoh an answer of peace." In other words he is saying, "There is nothing special about me; the living, True, personal God will give an answer when I communicate with Him." Joseph is saying God not only exists, but He will communicate with His children when they come to Him asking. Later when Joseph interprets the dream, he states clearly, "God has shown Pharaoh what he is about to do."

Joseph was thirty years old when he suddenly became second to Pharaoh in the land of Egypt, and had a position of being able to be a help to his own people when the terrible famine came. Here is a man who gives us a picture of one to come: a person rejected by his own, yet willing to go on to provide the help they needed. You know the story of the seven years of plenty, during which Joseph guided the Egyptians to grow tremendous crops and to store them carefully. You know the story of the seven years of famine, during which the stored up crops were sold so that people would not starve. You know the story of the brothers, the ten involved in selling Joseph, as they came down to Egypt to look for food, not having any idea that Joseph had lived and had become next to the Pharaoh of the land.

But come now and stand beside Joseph as he sees his brothers' faces for the first time in so many years. These are his people, but they have rejected him. He knows they need a lesson to bring understanding, but he hides away in another room to weep. As you weep with Joseph, overwhelmed with sudden emotion, remember another rejected one, the Messiah himself, years and years later, rejected, weeping as He says, "O Jerusalem, Jerusalem, how oft would I have gathered you as a mother hen her chickens, but you would not." A compassionate Joseph looks forward to the compassionate Messiah. Stand with Joseph later as he reveals himself to his brothers and comforts them in their fear of him because of what they have done. "Don't be angry or grieved with yourselves," he says. "You sold me for a wrong reason, but God sent me

SIX

to preserve your lives. God sent me before you to preserve you a posterity in the earth, and to save your lives by a great deliverance." Later in the Old Testament the psalmist sings in Psalm 105:17, "He sent a man before them, even Joseph who was sold for a servant: whose feet they hurt with fetters: he was laid in iron...."

The time comes when it is clear in Genesis 46:3 that God Himself has spoken to Jacob saying, "I am God, the God of thy father: fear not to go down into Egypt for there I will make thee a great nation: I will go down with thee into Egypt: and I will also surely bring thee up again: and Joseph shall put his hand upon your eyes."

And so Jacob and his entire family, numbering seventy now, come to have their need of food fulfilled. And we are told Joseph nourished his father, and his brethren, and all his father's household with bread. There is a picture here of a vivid enough sort to give those who look back at it some fresh understanding. Joseph is brought out of prison and out of death to provide bread, to give life, to those who had before rejected him. There is enough of a parallel here to bring thoughts to our minds who know now about the substitution of the lamb for atonement, so that there can be an awareness of a connecting thread of increasing understanding being unraveled. Joseph unfolds something of what the Messiah will do when He comes to give the bread of life, and the water of life, through His willingness to go on to help the "family members" of Israel in spite of their rejecting Him.

This brief study of Joseph's experience is needed to prepare the way for the next titanic moment of immediate need of the people of Israel, and for the next titanic moment in setting forth a new, fresh, vivid point of understanding of the meaning of coming to God with the lamb.

For four hundred years the people of Israel had been in Egypt. A new Pharaoh came to the throne, one who did not know Joseph, and who did not know what he had done for Egypt. All he knew was that this alien group of people who had arrived in the country so long ago as a family of seventy, now numbered over a million, counting women and children. Wanting to squash them out, this Pharaoh made their lives bitter with hard work in making brick, and in all manner of hard work in the fields. He even tried to murder boy babies at birth by telling the Hebrew midwives to kill boy babies when they came forth, but the midwives really feared God, and didn't do this. After that comes the time of commanding boy babies to be thrown in the river, and the marvelous story of Moses being cared for by his mother who prepared the wee boat to rock gently in the bulrushes with its precious cargo of one small boy baby. It was the Egyptian princess, Pharaoh's daughter, who had love for this baby, and who saved Moses to bring up as her own son.

We must rush on, however, to the time when God spoke to Moses, now eighty years old, out of the midst of a bush that burned brilliantly but was not consumed. God's direct message to Moses was that He had heard the cries of the Israeli people, and He had seen the oppression of the Egyptians, and that now was the time when they *must* be allowed to go free.

"How will the people know that you, God, have told me this? Who am I, to go to Pharaoh and tell him I am going to take the children of Israel out of Egypt? Also, how will the children of Israel have any confidence in me?"

God replies to Moses, "Thus shalt thou say unto the children of Israel, The Lord God of your fathers, the God of Abraham, the God of Isaac, and the God of Jacob, hath sent me unto you: ... this God hath said, 'I will bring you up out of the affliction of Egypt unto the land flowing with milk and honey....' "

God promises Moses that He will do "wonders," miracles, which will prove to the people that He, God, is the One who has sent him. Moses complains that he is not eloquent, he is not a speaker, and in the end God appoints Aaron as the mouthpiece of Moses.

Exodus 4:30, 31 gives us the first step of freedom, as we are told, "Aaron spake all the words which the Lord had spoken unto Moses, and did the signs in the sight of the people. And the people *believed:* and when they heard that the Lord had visited the children of Israel, and that he had looked upon their affliction, then they bowed their heads and worshiped."

SIX

Now the children of Israel are ready for the Lord to work in giving a solution to their bondage, in opening the way to freedom for them, as they have believed His word. There follows the story of Moses and Aaron going time after time before Pharaoh to ask that the children of Israel might be allowed to go into the wilderness to serve the Lord God. Each time a plague comes upon Egypt when Pharaoh refuses to let the people go. In the statement, "The Lord hardened Pharaoh's heart" it seems to me we have a clear picture of the fact that God is not going to allow Pharaoh to deceive the people. Government heads sometimes do one thing openly, while planning in hidden places to make a surprise attack; or they say one thing and even while saying it *know* that they have fooled the people as to what is "behind scenes." God was not allowing Pharaoh to act contrary to the reality that was there. Had the people been allowed to go a short distance, they could have been overtaken and punished by Pharaoh very easily. God is allowing the plagues from one to nine to prepare Pharaoh really to let the people go when the tenth plague fell!

Moses is told to tell Pharaoh what the tenth plague will be. "Thus saith the Lord, About midnight will I go out into the midst of Egypt: and all the firstborn in the land of Egypt shall die, from the firstborn of Pharaoh who sitteth upon the throne, to the firstborn of the maidservant that is behind the mill, and even the firstborn of the beasts."

There is time given for a decision on the part of Pharaoh, but the false Pharaoh is not allowed to make a false decision which will not only in the end harm the Israelites, but which will prevent a very important miracle from being shown so that all who see or hear of it, will *know* that the living God is God indeed.

It has been a long time since Abraham and Isaac went up the mountain together to worship God, and to be shown what the substitution of the ram meant. The Israelites have lived for a long time in the midst of a heathen nation who not only have not known their God, but who would not have any idea of what it would mean to have sin atoned for in any manner. The Israelites need a very definite and strong demonstration of what it means to come to God through the lamb, and they need reassurance also that God really is there, and will keep His promises to them.

The Jews now are going to be removed from slavery, but also from all that is familiar, and they need a very striking reality of the fact that they are truly God's people, being led by God who is able to care for them and their needs. They need to be reminded of the power of the infinite God, but also they need fresh understanding of *how* to come to Him. There would have been many temptations in the heathen culture based on the line of unbelief stemming from Cain, to turn away from the way of Abel, Noah, and Abraham. It would be surprising if some of them had not been a bit mixed up. Now at the very moment of their tremendous step out of Egypt and into the wilderness, following Moses and Aaron as they lead them into God's plan for them, they are to have something which will not only refresh their memory of what had been taught by Abraham but will take them one step further into understanding what it means to come to God with the lamb as their substitute.

In Exodus 12 the history of what happened is told, a history that is relevant to us, as well as to all the centuries of people who have lived since that important month. "And the Lord spake unto Moses and Aaron in the land of Egypt saying, This month shall be unto you the beginning of months: it shall be the first month of the year to you. Speak ye unto all the congregation of Israel, saying...."

What was it Moses was to tell the people so carefully, as God's direct word to them? It was something they needed to believe was true, and then act upon!

You are to take a lamb, one for each household. If your household is too small for a lamb, then share one among two or more households. This lamb must be without blemish, a perfect one, a male of the first year. You must keep it and watch it to see if it develops any blemish or not. If it is a splendid lamb, then on the fourteenth day of the month it must be killed in the evening.

Years later the Jew, Peter, was to write, "You know you

SIX

were not redeemed with corruptible things such as silver and gold ... but with the precious blood of Christ as a lamb without blemish and without spot."

Jesus had lived among men, had been tempted, had been tested, and was found without sin, even as the lambs were without blemish that night when the fourteen days of testing time were over, the eve of the terrible plague of death of the firstborn in Egypt, so many years ago.

After the lamb for each household was killed that evening, something else had to be done. The blood had to be caught in a basin and then carried to the door of the home. It was not enough that the lamb had died. For the death of the lamb to be effective in protecting the household, the blood needed to be applied to the two door posts at the side of the door, and to the upper post above the doorway.

But *why?* Because that night the Lord declared that He would mete out judgment to Egypt, against all the false gods of Egypt. Here is a group of people believing false teachings and worshiping false gods. The living God did not say, "These are different ways of worshiping me"; He said these were false gods, even as He said at other times in the Old Testament. Even as later in the time of Elijah God showed the priests of Baal that their gods had eyes but could not see, ears but could not hear, were being called upon but were powerless to answer. Even as God made clear to those watching that day when Elijah called out to Him, that He *did* hear, *could* answer, and had *power* to send down fire to consume the sacrifice—so this night in Egypt God was making the reality of His holiness and judgment known. "I am the Lord," he said, "and the blood shall be a token upon the houses where you are: and when I see the blood, I will *pass over* you, and the plague shall *not* be upon you to destroy you when I smite the land of Egypt."

This was a confrontation. It was not only a confrontation of Pharaoh against Moses, Moses against Pharaoh, but a confrontation of the true and living God against the false gods of Egypt. Who was strongest? Who really was the *true* God? What after all was *true?*

Was faith needed that night? Yes, the kind of faith Abel

needed. The kind of faith Abraham needed. Belief that God had spoken that which was true fact. The children of Israel, the Jews that night, needed to believe that God had spoken, and needed to act upon that belief.

"Father do you think it is necessary?" some boy might have asked, that dark Egyptian night in the warm, heavy air. "What good do you think blood will do on the doorposts?"

Perhaps one father replied, "Moses has told us that God said to do this or otherwise you, my son, and the eldest sons of any others who refuse to believe this to make a difference, will die at midnight tonight."

There may have been a lot of discussion. However the demonstration that proved the importance of acting upon God's command, was soon to be a vivid one, never to be forgotten. Do you suppose the families who awakened to hear the Egyptians screaming out because of the death of their sons, ever forgot the sound of those wails? Do you suppose the mothers and fathers who had believed, and had carefully chosen a lamb, killed it, and put the blood on the doorposts, *ever* forgot the result of finding their sons safe and well in the morning? Do you suppose the sons who were alive because the lamb had died, ever forgot the reality of what had taken place?

They were to roast the lamb before they went to sleep that night, and to eat it, roasted with fire, with unleavened bread, and with bitter herbs. Nothing was to remain of it in the morning. The command was given, "And thus shall ye eat it: with your loins girded, your shoes on your feet, your staff in your hand; and ye shall eat it in haste: it is the Lord's passover."

As they ate it they were ready to go out soon after and be pilgrims in a wilderness. It was a complete picture of something coming in the future. One day the promised Messiah was to die. He was to be the spiritual food to be fed upon, after the blood was "applied" through belief in what He had done. And those who would understand, believe, apply the blood, and feed on Him spiritually, were to be ready to be pilgrims in the wilderness of life's wanderings, before reaching an eternal land.

Fanciful? Not at all. Simply the detail-perfect picture of a

58

SIX

detail-perfect God. The Lord did not leave His people—nor any others who cared enough to seek Him with all their hearts—without understanding. In each moment of history there was sufficient knowledge given in order that the ones believing might act upon that belief, and come through the lamb pointing ahead.

Yes, the Lord passed through Egypt that night, and any house that had the blood on the doorposts was passed *over,* and no one died in these houses. The lambs had died, but the sons were alive. The clear picture was being given that an important understanding might result in years of waiting which were ahead. Someone was coming who would be the promised seed of the woman. Someone was coming who would have victory over death. This One would die, that others might live forever. The lesson of the Passover night was to extend into days, weeks, months, and years of discussion with enough "content" or factual explanation of history, to make it understandable. That which had been shown to Abraham and Isaac was now becoming more clear.

Now a command is given that the people may continue to think of the facts that were unfolded to them that night. The command is that they must remember (one's memory is in one's mind, hidden away), and *do* something outwardly to show forth the inward memory. They were to celebrate the Passover every year at the same time. The Passover was not to become just a religious festival for the sake of a holiday, but it was to be a very serious reminder of what had taken place, and a time of expressing belief in the manner of bringing a sacrifice which would look ahead to the coming Messiah who would take them to a promised land which would be permanent rather than temporary. In the book of Hebrews we are told that although Moses trembled when he came to the mountain where he was to receive the ten commandments, there is a day in the future when we are to come to Mount Sion, and unto the city of the living God, the heavenly Jerusalem, and to an innumerable company of angels—and to Jesus, the mediator of the new covenant, and to the blood of sprinkling, that speaketh better things than that of Abel.

Yes, there is a remembering of the important history of
the Passover to be carefully carried out through the centuries.
Year after year as the children ask, "What do you mean by this
service?" the parents are meant to say, "It is the sacrifice of the
Lord's passover, who passed over the houses of the children
of Israel in Egypt...." The children were to be given a clear
understanding of what it was all about, generation after
generation.

Exodus 12:42: "It is a night to be much observed unto the
Lord for bringing them out from the land of Egypt: this is that
night of the Lord to be observed of all the children of Israel in
their generations."

There was meant to be not just an outward observance of some
"religious rites" but as generations went on, people were
meant to discuss, talk about, explain, give understanding, to
their children and their children's children all that they had been
told, and all that they had experienced. In Deuteronomy 6:5, 6, 7
Israel is being commanded to hear that the Lord is one Lord and
that "thou shalt love the Lord thy God with all thine heart, and
with all thy soul and with all thy might. And these words, which
I command thee this day, shall be in thine heart: and thou
shalt teach them diligently unto thy children, and shalt talk of
them when thou sittest in thine house, and when thou walkest
by the way, and when thou liest down, and when thou
risest up."

Yes, the ten commandments are given in the next few verses,
and the commandments are being spoken of, but it is far more
than that. Children are meant to be considered important,
significant human beings, made in the image of God. They are
meant to be communicated with, in great sections of time when
parents are walking with them, sitting with them, eating with
them, and continually discussing, answering questions,
being interested. The picture given here is not one of an empty
house and broken relationships. The word of God, the
commandments of God, and the solution of how to come to
God are meant to be naturally the central knowledge to be
imparted from father to son, mother to daughter, parent to
child, generation to generation, in precious hours day after day.

SIX

"And when thy son asketh thee in time to come saying, What mean the testimonies and the statutes, and the judgments which the Lord our God hath commanded you? Then thou shalt say unto thy son, We were Pharaoh's bondmen in Egypt: and the Lord brought us out of Egypt with a mighty hand."

Yes, the picture of the doorposts splashed with blood, the sound of the Egyptian wails, the safety of the ones who slept in a real sense "covered by the blood," safe from death, the eating of the roasted lamb, the readiness to go out into the wilderness, the miracle of crossing the Red Sea, the continual leading of the Lord by a pillar of fire at night, and a cloud in the daytime ... all this was to be made vivid to the generation which had not experienced it. The only way one generation, the one that follows a tremendous moment of history, can find out about it and be aware of what it means to them personally, is to have it handed down verbally.

By word of mouth God has kept alive the content of truth which Satan tried to stamp out. By recorded words on stone, parchment, and paper, God has unfolded all the facts of past history we need to know, all the essential teaching we need to have, all the understanding of how we are meant to get rid of sin and how we may come into His presence, become His people, look forward to a time of complete restoration. God has been fair with us to leave more than the "works of His hands" through which to find out about Him. "The heavens declare the glory of God and the firmament showeth his handiwork," we are told. We should know He is there by seeing evidence of His creation, just as thoroughly as we are certain of an artist's existence through the works of his hands. However we are given opportunity to know more than His existence. We are given the way by which we may come to know Him personally now, and the way by which we can one day have victory over the death which would separate us from life forever with Him. All this He has verbalized for us, because we are verbalizing creatures. All this He has given in an understandable way, because we have been given minds with which to reason and understand.

Faith is not a mystical something that hits us like lightning. Faith comes by *hearing,* so we are told, and hearing comes by the word of God.

As the Egyptians pursued from behind—for they did come dashing after the children of Israel with their chariots of war—and as the Red Sea loomed up ahead, the Lord demonstrated to Israel, and to the jeering Egyptians, once more that He was God indeed. But first He said through Moses to the people, in words they should never have forgotten, and which come to us today as God has meant them to in recording them in the Bible, "Stand still, and see the salvation of the Lord, which he will shew to you today: for the Egyptians ye have seen today, ye shall see them again no more." That day the Israelites saw the Red Sea piled up on itself in great sea walls of water with a dry road between for them to walk over—a million, with women and children. Is it hard for the God who is Creator of the universe to push back the water of His own creation for His people to be given a safe passage? The experience of walking between those walls was to impress the people with the truth of God's strength and power. As the Egyptians plowed right ahead on that road between the walls of water, the water came in with a rush. God simply removed the miracle and the sea went back to its normal position.

They had seen the salvation of the Lord from the death of the firstborn because they had fulfilled his command to use the blood of the lamb as a sign of their believing. Now they are told to "stand still" in the face of the enemy who would try to kill the very much *alive* firstborn sons of Israel. At this command to "stand still," we who have David's Psalms, these songs written and sung by King David many years later, can think of these words in Psalm 20:5-9 with tremendous feeling for those who had escaped death by the blood of the lambs just the night before, and now were standing still, by the banks.

> *We will rejoice in thy salvation,*
> *and in the name of our God we will set up our banners:*
> *the Lord fulfil all thy petitions.*
> *Now know I that the Lord saveth his anointed:*

SIX

He will hear him from his holy heaven
with the saving strength of his right hand.
Some trust in chariots, and some in horses:
but we will remember the name of the Lord our God.
They are brought down and fallen:
but we are risen, and stand upright.
Save, Lord: let the king hear us when we call.

And in Psalm 102:

This shall be written for the generation to come:
and the people which shall be created shall praise the Lord.
For he hath looked down from the height of his sanctuary;
from heaven did the Lord behold the earth;
To hear the groaning of the prisoner;
to loose those that are appointed to death;
To declare the name of the Lord in Zion,
and his praise in Jerusalem.

Thank God these things of history and of truth were written
for the generations to come, because we are in that category, and
now we can follow the thread of continuity with understanding
and belief, so that it will be possible for our praise of God to
be *real* and not a hollow irrational hope, but a hope based on
truth.

SEVEN

The Exodus—The Second Book of Moses—is it *man's* writings?
A great man's ideas? No, history, prophecy of the future,
admonitions as to how to come into relationship with God,
how to continue to be close to the living God day by day—a
book to preserve the clear understanding of history from God's
viewpoint as well as to give the facts of history. A book for
God's people, the Jews, but for anyone to be able to read
through centuries, given by inspiration to Moses who also
was living through much of what he was writing about, as well
as being given knowledge and understanding far beyond
his own.

A million Jews. And babies being born daily. Imagine the
tents, the quiet at night being broken by a new baby's cry,
broken by the moan of someone with an attack of appendicitis.
Imagine the children squabbling together in the early morning
over some stick or stone they were claiming for a toy.
Imagine the women airing their sleeping pads, shaking out
clothing, combing their hair, gossiping with the ones in the next
tent. But what topics of very important conversation they had
been given! What terrific proof they had to talk about that
there was a true and living God who had freed them from the
whip and sweat of slavery! What endless wonder and excitement
they could have had as they related to each other their feelings
the night that the blood had been put on their doorposts.
Now what? There should have been an expectation and

waiting to see how God would lead next and how He would provide the immediate need.

What *was* the immediate need? First food and then water. Two essentials. Much unbelieving complaining started up among the tents, and was probably echoed by the children. "My daddy says we are going to starve." "Mom said Moses just brought us out here to be hungry." "I want something to eat *now*." Echoes of the adult unbelief—the adult criticism of God—would permeate the camp. Imagine some dear one behind a sheltering tree or tent flap perhaps praying, "O God, show them that you *are* real. Make them remember the Red Sea's power rushing over the Egyptians but *your* power in holding it back from us. O God, make them all believe the *truth* of the signs you have given us." Perhaps a woman prayed for her husband, for her children, to be *true* to the God of Abraham, Isaac, and Jacob.

But the majority were complaining, murmuring, and saying, "We would have been better off dead, than to be brought out here to starve!" And then the Lord said to Moses that He would rain bread, manna, morning by morning which would be *like* coriander seed, and would taste *like* wafers made with honey. Perhaps it was like a wheat germ, yoghurt, and honey mixture; surely it had all the right nutritive elements in it for the people and their children to be supplied with energy and the total of what proper food gives. Morning by morning people would swarm out of their tents. There was sufficient for everyone. In fact, if the people were greedy and took too much, any left over would go sour and moldy over night. No one lacked, and no one had too much. It was a perfect demonstration of how God means His people to be supplied, with no great store accumulated which depletes the supply for others.

Now remember, these people had already lived through the vivid experience of the lamb's blood saving their firstborn from death. They had already lived through the Red Sea experience. The supply of food dropping where all they had to do was to pick it up, with each one protected from having too little because of some weakness, was in addition to what had gone

before. It also is to be handed down to the generations
coming in the future. In Exodus 16:32 Moses said, "This is the
thing the Lord commandeth, Fill an omer of it [the manna] to be
kept for your generations; that they may *see* the bread
wherewith I have fed you in the wilderness when I brought
you forth from Egypt." The word was to be passed down by
mouth from father to son to grandson. The word was to be written
by Moses to be read over and over again through the years
ahead. The actual manna was to be supernaturally preserved
so that it could be *seen* by people not yet born, to be a proof to
them that all this was *true* history.

Remember that the lamb had been eaten after it was roasted
(after the blood had first been applied) to supply strength
for the journey ahead. Now the manna which was the daily
food had a double reason for being given. The lamb is always to
point forward to the Messiah who is one day to come and take
the place of those who need atonement. The manna is
another way of looking forward to a spiritual food which is also
to be *enough* for everyone who will gather it. This same Messiah is
to supply the spiritual food, or manna, day by day to those who
come believing. When He comes He is to say, to Jews who
had the books of Moses, who were meant to study them and
think about them day and night and to talk about them to their
children, "I am the bread of life."

Listen in detail as centuries later Jews ask, "What shall we
do that we might work the works of God?"

And Jesus answers carefully, "This is the work of God, that you
believe on him whom He hath sent."

Then they answered with this reference to the manna
which they knew so well, as they had been taught, "What sign
will you show us that we may see and believe you? ... Our fathers
did eat manna in the desert: as it is written [in the Scriptures],
He gave them bread from heaven to eat." Then Jesus
replied to them, "Verily verily, I say unto you, Moses gave you
not that bread from heaven; but my Father giveth you the true
bread from heaven. For the bread of God is he which cometh
down from heaven, and giveth life unto the world."

Jesus is explaining that the manna had a double reason for

being given. Jesus is pointing out that the Old Testament is history, as he refers to the bread Moses told about in Exodus, and He is also saying that there is a "bread of life" portrayed by the miracle of bread in the desert. In the desert of an abnormal world full of ugliness and death, *"The* Bread of Life" has been supplied, that people might eat, and have eternal life.

The Jews listened eagerly and replied, "Give us this bread." And then it was that Jesus said clearly, "I am the bread of life: he that cometh to me shall never hunger; and he that believeth on me shall never thirst."

Thirst?

Go back to the wilderness. The next subject of complaining and murmuring was rumbling through the camp. "We want water!" It was something like an ugly mob voice screaming today for some kind of "rights," ready to riot. This time another miracle with a double importance of central teaching was done before the eyes of all the people. The ugly rising roar must have turned to whispers of awe or shrill notes of surprise.

Moses was told by the Lord to go on before the people, to take the elders of Israel with him, and to stand before a rock. The same rod with which he had gone before Pharaoh was to be taken in his hand, and he was to hit the rock with it—just *once.* The result was to be that water would immediately *gush* forth out of the rock, a supply sufficient for the whole million and more people to have their thirst quenched—a terrific miracle, proving that God is God indeed, reassuring the Jews that it was the true and living God who was with them, and leading them. Reason enough that water was supplied, and that people were reassured? Well, in addition there was a *strong memory* to be passed down from generation to generation. So that when Jesus was later to say, "I am the water of life, he that believeth on me shall never thirst," it was meant to be *enough* to prove that He was indeed the Messiah. Come to the Jew Paul, whom we will talk about later. Just now, simply look at what he is saying to Jews in Corinth in 1 Corinthians 10:1-4: "I don't want you to be ignorant, brethren, how that all our fathers were under the cloud, and all passed through the sea; and were all baptized unto Moses in the cloud and in the sea; and did all eat

SEVEN

the same spiritual meat; and did all drink the same spiritual drink: for they drank of that spiritual Rock that followed them: and that Rock was Christ." And in verse 11, "Now all these things happened unto them for examples."

Yes, in a particular point in history, and all through the centuries, men were given a demonstration, a reality of God's existence, both to look back upon, and to look forward to, and to experience with *understanding* that they might *know*.

Can we say, "Oh, well, people forget after a long time goes by." Look how quickly and impatiently people turn away from sufficient evidence. It isn't that there is something wrong with the evidence. Nor that there is any shift in the "way" being explained. The continuity is fantastic. Moses was to strike the rock—once. Jesus was "struck" once; that is to say, He died once. God has given a continuity in His events in history, in His illustrations and examples, that can be recognized. God's clear truth is not masked in shrouds of religious gobbledegook nor in mystical incantations understood only by the initiated. The Jews were given sufficient understanding for their own moment of history, and the record handed down gave continuity which was meant to prepare people to recognize events as they came to pass. We now have sufficient explanation to give us assurance and comfort in the present, and hope and expectation for the future.

But we don't have to jump up to *today* to illustrate men's turning away from God's true truth. It must have been within a disappointingly short time that watching angels or Jewish believers observed that a titanic turning away took place. Moses had gone up a mountain, leaving Aaron and the elders below with the people. Moses had received the ten commandments, and had been given specific plans for the tabernacle. Moses had been told that two lambs were to be offered day by day, one in the morning, and one in the evening, at the door of the tabernacle, and God had promised to meet with him there, and had said, "I will dwell among the children of Israel, and will be their God. And they shall know that I am the Lord their God that brought them out of the land of Egypt, that I may dwell among them...."

But even as Moses was about to start down that long
mountain with the tablets of stone on which God had written
the ten commandments, an impatient, murmuring, complaining
mob of people were persuading Aaron to give them a *visible*
god to bow in front of. "Moses," they said, "has
disappeared, and we haven't a clue as to what has happened to
him." What a short patience! What an amazing turning away from
evidence! Men don't change much. Eve and Adam had the
words of God ringing in their ears, and all His perfect
creation all around them, but they turned to the lie rather than
the truth, and acted upon the lie! Abel believed and brought the
lamb so faithfully, but Cain, who had just as much opportunity
to know the truth, turned away and defiantly brought the
work of his hands. Now the million persuade Aaron, who
knew so thoroughly the power of God and who He was, to set up
a false god and to lead the people to the altar of Cain.

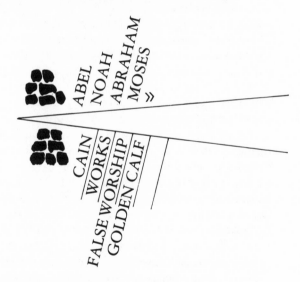

Can't you just picture all million strong shifting away
from the true line where they should have been looking toward
the Messiah with the lamb as their sacrifice, shifting down to
Cain's line bowing to an altar with a golden calf on it. Here

SEVEN

there is no living lamb dying for the needed understanding of a necessary atonement; here is a people-made god, made out of all the melted earrings, bracelets, necklaces which people had taken and thrown into a melting pot. Out comes a golden calf! And the label? The "name of God" was placed on this god. Shiny gold catching the sunlight, elegant and with no blood. Down go the heads, bowing as they brought peace offerings and burnt offerings and began to have a feast with dancing and playing, following this orgy of heathen worship. "These be thy gods, O Israel, which brought thee up out of the land of Egypt." What a melange! What a mishmash. What a confusion of words—words with a totally opposite connotation of their original meaning. What a lie! And Aaron is leading it as an outstanding example of all the false religious leaders who would say "words" with twisted meaning, who would take God's "Word," or words and put them in a different context, who would one day follow one another in leading people to bow before a variety of "golden calves," happy to find ways of leaving the altar of the bleeding lamb.

Is it any wonder that the Lord spoke of them as "a stiffnecked people" who needed punishment? But as Moses prayed and interceded for this people, asking God to remember His promises to Abraham, Isaac, and Israel, God answered his prayer, in giving the people another chance to repent. Moses then goes down to become very angry with Aaron as he hears his story and sees the people dancing naked before the calf. The story of the broken tablets, of the fighting breaking out, of the pleading of Moses as he asked God even to take his own place away, rather than cutting off all the people, is one which needs to be known to understand the compassion of God, as time after time He clarifies the fact that there is One God, and One Way to come to Him, and that all other gods are false, and lead completely away from Himself. Over and over again there are "confrontations" at which time the reality of true truth is made evident. Continually there is more history *behind* human beings, as proof, as well as hope, without a break, for the future.

The tabernacle is built, with details given by God to Moses.

The worship is always centered about the lamb. In the most holy place, behind a heavy, heavy curtain, the ark of the covenant—which is a box containing the tablets of the law, the rod, and the manna—has a lid, or a covering, which is called the propitiatory or "the mercy seat." Year after year the high priests following Aaron went into this holy of holies to sprinkle the blood of a lamb for the sins of the Jewish believers, on the lid, the mercy seat. Children's questions as to what this was all about were meant to be answered in full. There was supposed to be understanding. There was supposed to be a growing anticipation that the Messiah would come in person, to fulfill all that was pointing toward Him as the One who would be the real atonement.

When Moses died, God spoke to Joshua to carry on with this great promise of continuity. "Be strong and of good courage; be not afraid, neither be thou dismayed: for the Lord thy God is with thee whithersoever thou goest." Joshua believed the Lord, and prepared the people to be led by the Lord, by leading them in three days of fasting and prayer before they came to the edge of the Jordan River which was to separate *when* the priests stepped into it, carrying the ark, *believing* God's command. The belief was involved, and the act of stepping in the water, believing, and once more a dry path gave the Israelites a *way* in an impossible moment. Can't you imagine that the people's thoughts went back to the Red Sea? None of these would remember the Red Sea, except as small children, but they had heard enough day after day that this would tie in. And in case these very people might be careless in teaching *their* children, in Joshua 4:21-24 Joshua says very strongly: "And he spake unto the children of Israel, saying, When your children shall ask their fathers in time to come, saying, What mean these stones? [twelve stones taken out of Jordan to pile up as a memoriam] Then ye shall let your children *know*, saying, Israel came over this Jordan on dry land. For the Lord your God dried up the waters of Jordan from before you, until ye were passed over, as the Lord your God did to the Red sea, which he dried up from before us, until we were gone over: That *all* the people of the earth might know the hand of the Lord

that it is mighty: that ye might fear the Lord your God
forever."

Any who did not tell their children and their grandchildren
from generation to generation, of the marvel of the living God
and the way to come to Him in worship with the lamb—as
the day by day, morning and evening lamb was brought, or the
special Day of Atonement lamb was brought by the High
Priest—were depriving their children of knowing the truth. It
was the cruelty of parent to child, of grandparent to
grandchildren, of uncles to nieces and nephews, of aunts to
their sister's or brother's children. People have been deprived of
having a choice to believe by the ones of one generation
making a choice to not even bother telling them. All Jews
should have been told the clarity of Abraham and Isaac's
experience on the mountain, and of the whole of Israel's
experience as they took part in the first "passover" and went
free out of Egypt. All Jews should have been told what the
worship consisted of in the tabernacle, and later the temple.

It *is* clear—and thank God the Scripture has preserved it for us
because He did not allow His Word to be destroyed or deleted
out of existence. We now can still read and choose to
believe. Our opportunity has not been wiped out by selfish and
stubborn unbelievers as long as Scripture exists in so many
languages.

Come to Joshua's last charge to the Jews before he dies, as
he reviews the wonders of all God has done through the years,
and then cries out, "Now therefore fear the Lord, and serve him
in *sincerity* and in *truth,* and put away the gods which your
fathers served on the other side of the flood, and in Egypt
[Cain's line of false worship, in other words] and serve ye the
Lord....*Choose* you this day whom ye will serve: whether the gods
which your fathers served that were on the other side of the
flood, or the gods of the Amorites, in whose land ye dwell:
but as for me and my house, *we* will serve the Lord."

The people cried out that they did not want to serve any other
gods, but that they indeed would serve the Lord God who had
brought them out of Egypt. The choice of the people of
Israel that day was very strong, and we are told they *did* serve

the living God for all the rest of Joshua's life, and the time during which the elders lived, who were Joshua's helpers and had known the works of the Lord during his time.

How marvelous it would be had *everyone* who was born of the Israelites continued to know, believe, and act upon their belief through the centuries. Yet how marvelous it is that there were always some who *did* believe and continue in the stream of believers looking forward with hope to the fulfillment of all the promises God gave Abraham.

EIGHT

As we fly like a bird, an imaginary bird which can fly over time and space through the past, to see the continuity, the changelessness of the truth, and the constant egoism and stubbornness of *people,* it is tempting to scream, "Oh, *why* didn't more of them realize that they were selling their souls, their eternal lives, for a mess of pottage as Esau did?" You remember that Esau had a birthright that belonged to him, and he sold it for a momentary filling of a momentary hunger, as he accepted a steaming bowl of bean minestrone from Jacob in exchange for his precious birthright. Yes, as we fly over history as if it were a gigantic piece of tapestry and we see the continuity of that which God has woven in bright colors, we find it staggering to watch the choices men, women, and children have made. The truth was made plain to Adam and Eve. The truth again was plain for Cain and Abel. Noah preached his lungs out as he hammered away at the boat, giving a free invitation for others to join him in safety. Abraham saw it, and was willing to go out alone into the wilderness because he was convinced this was true, and he believed God.

Abraham was the first person to be circumcised as a mark of the covenant made with him. After that, every male child born in the line of Abraham, now called Jews or Israelites, was circumcised to show he was included in the covenant as one of God's people. But the circumcision did not protect them from making foolish choices. The circumcision was not magic. It was an outward sign that this boy had been born into the "line" of Abraham, but an inward belief was necessary to be in the eternal family of God.

It was made plain in Deuteronomy 10:12, 16, 19, 20 that circumcision was not magic nor were people left in any doubt of this way back there. Listen: "And now Israel, what doth the Lord thy God require of thee, but to fear the Lord thy God, to walk in all his ways, and to love him, and to serve the Lord thy God with all thy heart and with all thy soul.... Circumcise therefore the foreskin of your heart, and be no more stiffnecked.... Love ye therefore the stranger: for ye were strangers in Egypt. Thou shalt fear the Lord thy God; him shalt thou serve, and to him shalt thou cleave, and swear by his name."

Yes, it was always the inward *belief* that God's verbalized, understandable message was *true,* with day by day action and life exhibiting that fact, which counted. However, the outward sign of circumcision was an important sacrament in looking back to the covenant made with Abraham. It was an individual sign given to families through the males, that they were a part of the people of God, the people who worshiped the true, living God and not the gods of men's making, the people who came to their worship through a lamb, a substitute made clear when the ram was placed on the altar instead of Isaac. These circumcised people had the sign in their bodies that their parents had solemnly promised to teach them the truth of God's Word morning, noon, and night, and to tell them Passover day after Passover day what the blood of the lamb on the doorposts meant! A lot of people broke the promises they made about what they were going to teach those little eight-day-old baby boys! What a responsibility!

When anyone came to believe in the truth of the God of the Jews being the one real God of the universe, that person, if it was a man, became circumcised to show this fact. So some "outsiders" came into the *real* family through belief, while many circumcised ones shifted to Cain's line of unbelief.

In the New Testament when Paul, a Jew, is talking to other Jews, he says a lot of things in Romans 2 about circumcision.

EIGHT

Verses 28, 29: "For he is not a Jew which is one outwardly; neither is that circumcision which is outward in the flesh: but he is a Jew which is one inwardly; and the circumcision is that of the heart in the spirit, and not in the letter; whose praise is not of men, but of God." He goes on to ask if there is any advantage at all in being a Jew. His answer is that there is much advantage because Jews were committed to the oracles of God, that is, the teaching of God in the Bible. He says that just because some did *not* believe, that did not make the true belief to be canceled out. In other words, just because people say a thing is not true, and turn away scornfully, that does not affect reality or true truth one bit! What really exists, exists whether anyone believes it is there or not. The bump you get on your head from hitting the corner of a door is just as painful even if you say the door is not there!

Then Paul goes on to talk of those who *did* believe, starting with Abraham who he says believed. "He staggered not at the promise of God through unbelief but was strong in the faith, giving glory to God."

Happily there were many others of the circumcised ones through the centuries who were faithful to God, and who demonstrated their faithfulness in their coming to Him in the way He had made clear was the only way. Happily there was always a "remnant" to teach the next generation, and to stand up and have a confrontation with those who were giving a false teaching, and compromising with the worship of false gods.

It is important to note that the word "god" does not refer to the true and living God alone. All through the Old Testament God speaks to His people and uses the word "god" to point out that the word itself is not sufficient. The word "god" was attached to the golden calf, and to all the idols and concepts of men's imaginations throughout the centuries. True enough, there *is* only one real God, only one living God, only one Creator of the universe, only one Master of the universe—but everyone who uses the word "god" is *not* necessarily speaking of *Him.* God Himself uses the word "god" to refer to the false gods, to refer to the gods of men's invention. People often say that men have invented god, that men

have devised god as a basket into which to throw all their
problems, or as an aspirin pill to dim the pain of life. True
enough that men *have* invented gods to suit their own fancies.
True enough that men *have* created gods and whole systems of
worship of these gods. Men's ways of coming to these false
gods, and men's false ways of trying to come to the true
God, have one thing in common which puts them all on those
vertical parallel lines springing off from the line of Cain. What *do*
they have in common? It is the way of coming to please these
gods, or trying to please the real God, by the works of their
own hands—religious good works or moral good works.

The "remnant," the faithful circumcised ones, the ones who
continued to believe that God was speaking the truth when He
made it clear how to come to Him, were not at all confused
as to the continuity through the ages. In all periods of history
some believed so firmly that the promises and covenants of God
were true truth, that they had courage to stand "on the end of a
limb" so to speak, in the most terrifying places of danger.
These people believed God to be all-powerful and believed
that they were in communication with Him, and that He *could*
work in space and time and history—in *their* moment of history
and in their geographic location.

Look, as we fly hurriedly on, at Gideon. At his moment of
history the Israelites were being devastated by the Midianites
who were stronger and had a larger army. When God spoke
to Gideon and commissioned him to step out and lead a
counterattack to drive the enemy away, Gideon was amazed and
spoke of his own inability and weakness, and of his place as the
least in a family that was unimportant. He asked God for a
sign to be sure that it was God telling him to be leader, and God
very gently and patiently gave not just one sign, but several. Now
Gideon, convinced this was his task, gathered together an army
of 32,000 men to fight. But God wanted him to *know* that
God was doing a supernatural thing, and not to trust in the
strength of his gathered-together army. It was again the same
thing as the evidence given to Moses and then all the Israelites
at the Red Sea. There is proof to be given to all who will
look and seriously consider what is happening. The historical

EIGHT

evidence does several things at once. It reassures the believers who have taken a stand "on the end of a limb," certain that God is there and is leading them; it convinces some of the unbelievers that they are wrong and brings them to the true God; and it defeats Satan in a skirmish as it shows how powerless the false gods are.

What happened with Gideon? Well, after one "test" 22,000 soldiers turned and went home. After the next "test" all but 300 were eliminated. Now comes the "impossible": 300 men are to fight the hosts of the Midianites. Thrill once again, no matter how many times you have heard this story, with the wonder of what really took place. Three hundred men won the battle, hands down! How? By following God's strategy as God told Gideon to have them arranged in groups of one hundred on three hills surrounding the Midianite tents in the valley. It was the middle of the night. The three groups were armed with pitchers, lamps, and horns! The lamps were lighted but covered with pitchers so that the light did not show. At a given signal they broke the pitchers—crash! clatter!—blew blasts on their horns, and of course as the Midianites awakened groggy, rushing out of their tents to see what all the noise was, they were confused by the lights above, and rushed at each other. Yes, they defeated themselves as they fought each other in the dark. After the blast of the horns and the crash, the 300 shouted, "The sword of the Lord and of Gideon!" and, tumbling about in chaos, the enemy's men ran away fighting as they went, but fighting each other!

Many women are recorded as strong in their faith in the living God, and their stories are meant to also convince and strengthen others who hear, from generation to generation. Stop to look at Hannah praying in the temple as she asks for a son, and promises to give him in a special way to the Lord. And then listen to her prayer after Samuel is born. 1 Samuel 2: "And Hannah prayed, and said, My heart rejoiceth in the Lord, mine horn is exalted in the Lord.... There is none holy as the Lord: for there is none besides thee: neither is there any rock like our God." Her child grew to lead in the temple worship following the "understanding continuity." Listen to Samuel

years later as he has prayed for a miracle to convince men
that God is God indeed and to cry out to them to turn back,
back to the *real* line, away from the false. 1 Samuel 12:16: "Now
therefore stand and see this great thing which the Lord will do
before your eyes." And later, in verse 20: "...turn not aside
from following the Lord, but serve the Lord with all your
heart." And 23, 24: "Moreover as for me, God forbid that I
should sin in ceasing to pray for you: but I will teach you the
good and the right *way:* Only fear the Lord, and serve him in
truth with all your heart: for consider how great things he hath
done for you."

Very soon after this, Samuel is led by God to anoint an
unknown young shepherd boy in preparation for later being
the king. Come to the moment when this beautiful David, with
flushed cheeks and glowing eyes (as the most beautiful young
Jewish teen-ager you have ever seen) stands before the giant
Goliath who has been "troubling Israel." Just as with the
weak Israeli slaves leaving Egypt as chariots of war pursued
them, just as with Gideon's weak 300 standing in the starlight on
hills, about a huge sleeping army, here stands David before an
enormous giant in armor and with huge sword, with nothing
in his hand but a slingshot and five round stones! How
dramatic a confrontation!

Please listen to what David says as he stands there before the
sneering giant. Yes, you have heard it before, but consider
seriously now—ask yourself, "Has God been fair through the
ages? Has He made things clear to the Jews, and to any of the
watching world who care to look and consider seriously
whether God is really there?"

1 Samuel 17:45: "Then said David to the Philistine, 'Thou
comest to me with a sword, and with a spear, and with a shield: but
I come to thee in the name of the Lord of hosts, the God of the
armies of Israel, whom thou hast defied. This day will the
Lord deliver thee into mine hand; and I will smite thee, and
take thine head from thee; and I will give the carcases of the hosts
of the Philistines this day unto the fowls of the air and to the
wild beasts of the earth: that all the earth may *know that there
is a God in Israel.* And all this assembly shall know that the Lord

saveth not with sword and spear: for the battle is the Lord's and *he* will give you into our hands.' "

Yes, you've seen paintings, you've heard the story, you have a picture of that giant's head hit by the stone and then cut off as the lad stands beside the fallen enemy. But have you come to the conclusion, which is what it was all about? God recorded this happening in history, as well as causing it to be a vivid reality at the time, to let it be known that the truth is *true* and there is no change.

You sing the psalms of this King David. Perhaps the words are familiar to you, but what of the reality of what he says? Listen to Psalm 9:1: "I will praise thee, O Lord, with my whole heart: I will shew forth *all* thy marvelous works." Then verse 10, "And they that *know* thy name will put their trust in thee: for thou Lord, hast not forsaken them that seek thee." It is David who sings of the marvel of God's creation in Psalm 19. David who as a shepherd boy sat on hillsides under starry skies and watched the sun come up as he played his harp. "The heavens declare the glory of God, and the firmament sheweth his handiwork. Day unto day uttereth speech and night unto night sheweth knowledge." Yes, David looked at the beauty of starlight and moonlight lighting up meadows and trees, thinking of God the Artist. David watched sunrise and sunset, thinking of how it communicated the glory of the Creator of it all. This same David wrote Psalm 22 as God opened his understanding with inspiration such as only the writers of the Bible have had. In this Psalm he portrays the death of the coming Messiah. Just look at verses 17, 18, 19: "I may tell all my bones: they look and stare upon me. They part my garments among them, and cast lots upon my vesture. But be not thou far from me, O Lord: O my strength, haste thee to help me."

Yes, in this Psalm David was given by God one more piece of understanding as to the coming Messiah who would Himself be the Lamb, the atonement. He wrote and sang prophecies by inspiration, but the ones who would live at the time it all happened, and who had heard these words from Psalm 22 sung in the Temple Sabbath by Sabbath were given a "key" to open a

door of understanding, by the very fair Master of the
universe, the living God who loved His people and wanted
them to be prepared to recognize the moment of history so long
prepared for, *when* it arrived!

Understanding of what the lambs were pointing forward to,
was unfolded with more detail as centuries went on, but at *any*
point in history there was sufficient factual content given so
that people could become true "spiritual Israel with
circumcised hearts" rather than just physically a part of the Jewish
people. And there was no time when *some* did not really
believe, and no time when the truth was not being
proclaimed by someone.

Solomon, David's son, was the one who built the temple.
Before David died he charged Solomon to keep God's
commandments and walk in his ways and his laws "as it is
written in the law of Moses." So David is admonishing his son
to stay close to the *word* of God, the Scriptures, the first five
books of Moses. 1 Kings 2:4: "That the Lord may establish his
word which he spake concerning me saying, If thy children
take heed to their way, to walk before me in *truth* with all their
heart, and with all their soul, there shall not fail thee a man on the
throne of Israel." Solomon sinned and turned from the law of
God in many ways, but he did believe not only in the
existence of the God of Moses, but in coming to Him in the
one and only way, until he compromised.

What a breathless moment in the history of the Jewish
people when the Temple was complete in all its beauty, and
the places for worship with the lambs were ready for the priests
to begin. Picture the carrying in of the ark to the holy place! Now
no temporary tabernacle, but the Temple, the heart of
Jerusalem, to be the center for so many years ahead—to be
the scene of a fresh moment of understanding so much later.
Now hear the even tread, tread, tread, tread of the feet of the
elders and the priests as they walk in solemn line. 1 Kings 8:3:
"And all the elders of Israel came, and the priests took up
the ark. And they brought the ark of the Lord, and the
tabernacle of the congregation and all the holy vessels that were in
the tabernacle, even those did the priests of the Levites bring

EIGHT

up." It goes on to tell of Solomon and the priests and the people being gathered there for sacrifice of the sheep and oxen as the ark went in. A moment of great emotion for them all. The land was established. The Jews were in the promised land with their own Temple, and now the ark was being carried into the *most* holy place, that place behind the enormously heavy curtain, not to be seen by any eyes now except the High Priest as he would sacrifice on the Day of Atonement for all the years ahead—all the years that the blood of the lamb would be brought and sprinkled on the mercy seat until ... until ... the *true* Lamb of God would come and die. When would it be? No one knew. These were *all* to die without *ever* seeing the ark outside. But the blood of the little lambs taken in by the High Priest *once a year* would look back to Abraham's toiling up that hill with Isaac carrying the wood, and would look forward to someone coming who would toil up that same hill! What a moment!

I often wonder how much those who have gone on to wait, without their bodies, for the time of the resurrection, *can* follow history. I often wonder how much the angels know beyond what is actually taking place. But can't you imagine Abraham's interest in the Temple being established, in the final resting place of the ark with its covering and the golden cherubims above it, as now the "scene is set" for the central moment of history which is ahead. All eyes should be watching this holy of holies in a special way through the years. It was central in importance to believing Jews. Were the angels and those who had gone before able to hear Solomon's prayer of dedication? Did they thrill with the listening believers who were that day in the land of the living? God has preserved for us the words of that prayer, so that we may thrill with it too, and join in praying for our moment of history as we look back ... and forward.

Before praying, Solomon told of the fact that David his father had thought to build this house for the Lord, but that God had said David's son would be the one to do it. He told carefully of the fact that the ark was the central thing of importance, because it contained the tablets of stone with the law, and because "within it is the covenant which God had made with our fathers when he brought them out of the land of Egypt."

And Solomon prayed: "Lord God of Israel, there is no God like thee, in heaven above, or on earth beneath, who keepest covenant and mercy with thy servants that walk before thee with all their heart." The long prayer goes on, and in one place he asks, "...forgive the sins of thy servants and of thy people Israel, that thou teach them the good way wherein they should walk...." And in another he asks, "...and do according to all that the stranger calleth thee for; that all the people of the earth may know thy name, to fear thee as do thy people Israel."

And when Solomon came to the end of his praying, he stood up and raised up his arms and blessed Israel with this blessing in a loud voice: "Blessed be the Lord that hath given rest unto his people Israel, according to all that he promised there hath not failed one word of all his good promise, which he promised by the hand of Moses his servant."

If only Solomon had continued in the way he began. But unhappily he not only married many wives, but got entangled and compromised with the false gods of these women, diminishing the possibility of truth being understood by many who would otherwise have known it. The cruelty of parent to children whom they have promised to teach, the cruelty of generation to generation, of man to man when various kinds of compromise fuzzy up the truth, is always sad, in history as we look back, but sad at *this* existential moment too. Solomon had wisdom of a special sort, became prosperous and famous, and then got mixed up with all the wives who were pagan and worshiped in pagan temples. Judgment came upon his sin, and other people suffered. What about right now in our own moment of history? Generation after generation has suffered because someone became egotistical and selfish and turned away from caring what God's purpose for his or her life was meant to be, and couldn't care less whether it was fulfilled or not. This is true of those who are a part of God's people, and so their actions are even more devastating because of the contrast of what "might have been." Add to that the ones who rebel, and reject true truth and start counter campaigns on

EIGHT

Cain's line, and you have some understanding of the thick
fog that blots out the true truth from the "eyes" of men's
minds.

It is no wonder that as time went on, a fearful false worship
was entered into by a lot of Israel. This was during the time
of Ahab, and idolatry was taking place in the worship of Baal.

But thank God for Elijah who believed God, and had such a
strong certainty that God was speaking truth in His word, that
he had just as much courage to stand alone as Abraham,
Moses, and David had. His "aloneness" was different, but
God, who is a God of diversity, has made men to be individuals,
not machines, so one expects men, as well as their experiences,
to be different.

Come to a moment in the preparation of Elijah for his public
confrontation with the priests of Baal. Elijah is all alone in a
wilderness spot by a brook when he learns to trust God for
his morning and evening food in a time of famine and in a place
where there were no delicatessens with kosher pickels and bagels.
Elijah trusted the living God to feed him as He had promised
to do, with ravens bringing bread and meat in the morning
and again in the evening to drop at his feet. Ravens are birds
who steal food, and are not naturally likely to drop it. God was
providing in just as definite a way for this one man, as He had
when he caused the manna to drop down for the million!
God is a personal God and since He is also infinite, time is no
problem to Him, nor space, so He can care personally for each
one of His children, no matter how many or how few. Elijah
was a child of God, through believing and coming to God in
the right way, the only, one way. Many, many other Jews at that
time were *not* being cared for by God because they were
deliberately worshiping Baal, a horrible false god with a
terrible kind of heathen worship. When people say, "God
never dropped any food at my feet" they may be simply trying
to be funny, or they may be seriously asking a question. God has
promised to hear His children when they cry out to Him. Listen
to David in Psalm 20: "The Lord hear thee in the day of
trouble; the God of Jacob strengthen thee out of Zion:
Remember all thy offerings, and accept thy burnt sacrifice. Grant

thee according to thine own heart, and fulfill all thy counsel. We will rejoice in thy salvation and in the name of our God will we set up our banners: the Lord fulfill all thy petitions." Wait a moment, what is the "burnt sacrifice"? Where is the lamb? What has happened to the continuity with the days of Elijah and all who have gone before?

Going back to Elijah, come to the time when he courageously faces 450 prophets of Baal on Mount Carmel, in front of all the children of Israel. The confrontation is one of placing the true and living God on one side and the god Baal on the other. Elijah is representing the God of Moses, and the 450 prophets are representing Baal. 1 Kings 18:21: "And Elijah came unto all the people, and said, How long halt ye between two opinions? If the Lord be God follow him, but if Baal then follow him. And the people answered him not a word. Then Elijah said unto the people, I, even I only remain a prophet of the Lord: but Baal's prophets are four hundred and fifty men." Elijah then calls for a test. He says two altars are to be built, and on each altar a bullock placed. There is to be no fire placed on the altars and the prophets are to call on Baal to send fire down, and he, Elijah, will call on the living God to send fire. The God who sends down fire will be proven to be the true God. And the people all said, "This is well spoken." In other words, "Great idea ... we'll do it."

The prophets of Baal had the first turn. They called from morning until evening and nothing happened. They jumped around in a frenzy and cut themselves with knives, but nothing happened. Elijah mocked them about noontime, saying, "Call a little louder, maybe he is asleep, or perhaps he went on a journey." This went on until time for the evening sacrifice, and nothing had happened; no voice was even heard.

Then Elijah gathered everyone around and made an altar of twelve stones. Why twelve? Representing the tribes of Israel, of course. Our God is a God of continuity. We are not allowed to get mixed up! Things fit together over the centuries.

Now in addition to the dry stones Elijah made a ditch and filled it with water, and even poured water over the bullock,

EIGHT

to make the test more complete. Then Elijah prayed and said, "Lord God of Abraham, Isaac, and of Israel, let it be known this day that thou art God in Israel, and that I am thy servant, and that I have done all these things at thy word. Hear me, O Lord, hear me, that this people may *know* that thou art the Lord God, and that thou hast turned their heart back again." He asked for a titanic request in asking for the fire, but a more titanic result. Elijah is asking that the result will be a turning back to God on the part of those who have really rejected Him, and that their turning back will be on the basis not of an emotion, but a *knowing* with their intelligent understanding that God is really there.

Then? Then? Then the fire of the Lord fell. True history is being given, not just "religious truth," but historic truth! The fire fell, and the burnt sacrifice was consumed. There was such heat that it just disappeared, and the wood and stones and dust, let alone the water, which the Bible tells us was "licked up." Yes, a heat came with the flames which demonstrates with an awesome demonstration the fact that God can speak a word and anything can happen, from fire coming down, to a storm ceasing. The God of Abraham, Isaac, Jacob, Joseph, David, and Elijah is the Master of the universe indeed. And when the people saw what took place, they fell on their faces—7000 of them—and worshiped saying, "The Lord he is God, the Lord he is the God."

Elijah is someone special indeed, because later he was taken to heaven in a fiery chariot. He did not die. He was not separated from his body, but he is one along with Enoch, who is in heaven in his body. The Bible tells us that Elijah is coming back someday in a very important moment in future history, and at that time he will be set upon and killed by those who will hate his preaching. However that is yet to come. What took place as Elijah went off before Elisha's astonished eyes, is that Elisha caught Elijah's "mantle" or cloak, and took Elijah's place as a faithful prophet.

You see the continuity continues, in the past, present, and future, and although we might like to simply sit in a stadium, or a theater, and watch as lights go up and down and curtains shut off part of the history or the prophecy, and then separate to give us clear glimpses of other parts, as onwatchers, as an audience being amused or even emotionally involved, and then put on our capes or coats and go out into the midnight air and wash away the remains of emotion with a cup of coffee bringing us back to "reality," we *can't*. Why? Because *if* it is *true* then *we* are a part of it all. We are a part of this moment of history, where this moment fits in to the whole scope. We are either one of the ones who are among the believing people of God, spiritual descendents of Abraham, or we are on one of the lines shooting off Cain's line, rebelling against coming to any god at all, or making up our own religions or ways of coming. That is *if* this is true truth which the Old Testament gives and the living God *is* the Creator who made man in His own image, a Person making people who are significant in a significant history.

The alternative is a universe totally operating like a machine, impersonal and determined, with no choice involved.

It is worth taking time to consider as we go on.

NINE

Elisha did believe and speak courageously. God gave him power to do many miracles that men might realize that what he was saying was truth, and listen with their whole beings. It was Elisha who was given the power to cause an ax-head to float so that it could be found; to heal a leper who was a captain of the Syrian host, but who came to Elisha because of a little Israeli serving maid who had courage to speak about God and His prophet. It was Elisha who prayed that food be multiplied for the feeding of a hundred men, so that twenty loaves of barley and some corn multiplied into sufficient to have some left over. It was Elisha who prayed and asked God to open his servant's eyes, and God answered. Do you know that story? Elisha and his servant were surrounded with enemy chariots and horses and the servant was afraid. When God answered Elisha's prayer, the servant's eyes were opened to see the *other* part of the real universe, and he saw what had been invisible before: he saw the mountain was full of horses and chariots of fire, and realized Elisha had been right when he said, "Fear not: for they that be with us are more than they that be with them" (2 Kings 6:16).

Yes, time after time in history, one or many who believed were given understanding and courage to make the truth known ... and *some* were always affected and came to the conviction that "the Lord He is God," while others sneered or laughed with scorn, or made up a counter-explanation of beginnings, endings, of how to live, and what life's purpose is.

Hezekiah was the king during the time of Isaiah, and Hezekiah really believed. Listen to his prayer in 2 Kings 19:14-19: "And Hezekiah received the letter of the hand of the messengers, and read it: and Hezekiah went up into the house of the Lord and spread it before the Lord, and said, O Lord God of Israel, which dwellest between the cherubim, thou art the God, even thou alone, of all the kingdoms of the earth; thou hast made heaven and earth. Lord, bow down thine ear and hear: open, Lord, thine eyes, and see: and hear the words of Sennacherib which hath sent him to reproach the living God. Of a truth, Lord, the kings of Assyria have destroyed the nations and their lands, and have cast their gods into the fire: for they were no gods, but the work of men's hands, wood and stone, therefore they have destroyed them. Now therefore, O Lord our God, I beseech thee, save thou us out of his hand, *that all the kingdoms of the earth may know that thou art the Lord God, even thou only.*"

It was prayer for another confrontation, that the power of the living God might be seen as He protected Israel, when the heathen gods had been resistless and powerless to prevent themselves from being set on fire. Another confrontation of a different sort, but similar to Elijah asking that the Baal worshipers be shown that Baal was no god at all. The prophet Isaiah was the one who received word from God as to His answer, and it was Isaiah who took the message that God had said, "And the remnant that escaped out of the house of Judah shall yet take root downward and bear fruit upward... For I will defend this city to save it for mine own sake and for my servant David's sake." And it came to pass that night that the Assyrian army was wiped out by the angel of the Lord. For the Lord's sake? That men might *know* that He indeed is God, and that the gods of men's making are no gods at all. For David's sake? That the descendants of Abraham, Isaac, and David might continue to have promises fulfilled.

What was the covenant made with Abraham and handed on down the line? In Genesis 12:1-3 God told Abraham that He

NINE

would make of him a great nation, and would bless him and make his name great, and "in thee shall all the families of the earth be blessed." It is important to keep this promise in mind through history. *How* are all the families in the earth to be blessed through Abraham's family? It unfolds century by century. There is Someone coming, a Messiah. He is to be born of the line of Abraham, Isaac, Judah, David, and although He was promised to Eve and Adam already, and pointed forward to by all the lambs, the narrowing down of family line is very specific.

What has this to do with Hezekiah's protection from the Assyrian army? A lot. Hezekiah believed God, and lived to a certain degree by prayer as we found him when he was so ill, praying for more years to live, and the Lord answered and promised him fifteen more years. Hezekiah knew Isaiah. Remember that Isaiah is not an airy-fairy, nebulous religious figure, he is fixed in a moment of history living in Hezekiah's period, but God gave him inspiration, knowledge of future events, so that he could speak and write the prophecies which are still so important to us today. Isaiah is as important to us as he was to Hezekiah, and he was as important to every period of history between that and this one.

If men in those days had only *read* and *believed* what God unfolded or revealed through Isaiah, they would have been prepared to recognize events as they took place. If men today would stop trying to invent several Isaiahs and destroying the supernatural of what God gave him to reveal, and rather take seriously the content of what they have been given, they would also be more prepared to recognize true truth now, and to wait with expectation that which God has promised ahead, being aware that some of the prophecies of Isaiah are already fulfilled but some are yet future.

Chapter fifty-three starts out with a question. "Who hath believed our report?" Who indeed! "And to whom is the arm of the Lord revealed?" Ah! To any who will listen with ears and minds. To any who will read with eyes and an ordinary understanding of words and grammar. Isaiah is going to go on and reveal something that God has made plain to him to

91

reveal that people may have another portion of understanding concerning the central thing in their worship. The lamb is brought morning and evening by priests. The lamb's blood is taken into the holy of holies once a year by the High Priest, to atone for the sins of the people, to demonstrate the need of substitution. Now Isaiah is going to make more clear the reality of what is coming that the believing Jews may recognize it when it *does* take place.

Forget for a moment that you have ever read Isaiah before. Forget for a moment whatever you have been taught by critics that Isaiah never wrote all of Isaiah and that this couldn't have been written 700 years before Christ. Forget that which men have said as they have taken the scissors of their unbelieving minds and have slashed out the supernatural parts of the Bible, letting them fall to the floor or in the fireplace, leaving a shorn bit of lacy scrap to piece together in the bizarre combinations their own minds imagine to make more sense. Forget that anyone has told you that the Bible is myth and fable and that therefore you can't intelligently be excited about it, and come to this passage with an open mind, letting it be understood easily because of what it says, instead of allowing it to become complicated by what people say it can't say.

"And when we shall see him, there is no beauty that we should desire him." This coming One is described as a man who will not look special, who will not stand out as a handsome, desirable person, nor have a magnetic personality of a leader. "He is despised and rejected of men; a man of sorrows and acquainted with grief: and we hid as it were our faces from him; he was despised and we esteemed him not." Isaiah is, seven hundred years before the Messiah comes, identifying the people and himself in the "we" who rejected the Messiah later. Isaiah is portraying what will happen, but in such a vivid way that the people who lived during the time that Christ was actually being rejected, should have been jolted to a recognition—and some were. The reaction should have been on the part of many—just as those fellows reacted when I read this passage in St. Louis back in 1947. The year is of no importance—B.C. ... A.D.—few or many years one side or the

NINE

other, the reality of what is being said is vividly
recognizable.

"Surely he hath borne our griefs, and carried our sorrows; yet
we did esteem him stricken of God, and afflicted. But he was
wounded for our transgressions; he was bruised for our
iniquities: the chastisement of our peace was upon him: and
with his stripes we are healed." Clear? Very clear to a people who
know something about the atonement from Moses' time on
through the day once a year when they were aware of it over
and over again throughout a lifetime. Clear that someone
being looked forward to, the Messiah, would come and take
the punishment for all the people. He would be bruised for
the sins of others. He would be chastised for other people's
peace. He would be beaten with "stripes" and because of that
the people could be healed, spiritually and eventually
physically.

But go on: "All we like sheep have gone astray, we have
turned every one to his own way; and the Lord hath laid on
him the iniquity of us all." Here people are identified with
sheep. All the Jews, all the family of God, are called sheep in the
way they wander off in a senseless fashion, looking for other
pastures in dangerous cliff-like spots. Sheep going astray,
away from the shepherd. Sheep needing a shepherd. We think
of the story of one lost lamb, and ninety-nine sheep in the fold,
and of the shepherd going out to be torn with thorns and cut by
brambles, leaning over the dangerous cliff to pick up the
lost sheep in his arms to carry it back to the fold. Then listen to
John, a Jew who much later wrote down some of the things the
Messiah said about himself, in John 10: "I am come that they
might have life, and that they might have it more
abundantly. I am the good shepherd: the good shepherd giveth
his life for the sheep."

Ah, but now back to Isaiah as he points forward: "He was
oppressed, and he was afflicted, yet he opened not his
mouth: he is brought as a lamb to the slaughter and as a sheep
before her shearers is dumb, so he openeth not his mouth."

Could it be more clear? The Messiah is to be the *Lamb*. The
Messiah is the one promised from the time of Eve and

Adam. The Messiah, promised to all the Jews from Abraham on, the one whom all the little lambs represented is to be *the Lamb*. His atonement for the sins of the people is pointed forward to with crystal clarity now. This is no mere man. This one is to die for the people, as the only one who could do it, and He is to be Himself the Lamb.

What a terrific switch—the Shepherd is to be the Lamb. The Lamb is the great Shepherd. Come back to David's song about the Shepherd, Psalm 23: "The Lord is my shepherd; I shall not want. He maketh me to lie down in green pastures: he leadeth me beside the still waters. He restoreth my soul: he leadeth me in the paths of righteousness for his name's sake. Yea, though I walk through the valley of the shadow of death I will fear no evil: for thou art with me; thy rod and thy staff they comfort me. Thou preparest a table before me in the presence of my enemies: thou anointest my head with oil; my cup runneth over. Surely goodness and mercy shall follow me all the days of my life: and I will dwell forever in the house of the Lord."

"The good shepherd giveth his life for the sheep." The shepherd is willing to become the Lamb. The one and only true Lamb of God is willing to be the substitute—not just for Isaac on Mount Moriah as the ram pointed forward, but now in reality for all Israel—for all the children of Abraham, who become a part of the family because of belief, and for all the "peoples of the earth to be blessed" as they too can come. Yes, the Shepherd who becomes the Lamb—the Son of God who becomes a Man—is able to be the substitute, so that the lost lambs, the lost people, can indeed have goodness and mercy follow them and can look forward to an everlasting life where they can dwell forever in the house of the Lord. David sang about it with a measure of understanding. Isaiah was given by God a more specific understanding of how it would take place.

Let us hurry on in Isaiah 53: "He was taken from prison and from judgment: and who shall declare his generation? for he was cut off out of the land of the living: for the transgression of my people was he stricken." Seven hundred years before the death of Christ, here is a description of his being taken from the judgment hall of Pilate to die—to be cut off out of the land of the living for the people. It is an atonement that is a substitution being described, to a people who were waiting outside the heavy curtain year after year on the yearly Day of Atonement. It fell into place. Isaiah writes on in further detail that which took place long after his own death, "And he made his grave with the wicked, and with the rich in his death; because he had done no violence, neither was there any deceit in his mouth." Here we can see why in St. Louis the Jewish student said, "Oh, that is Jesus Christ," without stopping to remember the date at which Isaiah wrote. Jesus *did* die between two criminals, and the grave that Joseph of Arimathea offered *was* the tomb of a rich man. He died not for any "violence" or "deceit" of his own; He was the Son of God, the Messiah who alone *could* be a substitute. He was the perfect Lamb without a single blemish—no lies had been in His mouth. Isaiah said it would be like this. Moses had said to the children of Israel that night in Egypt that the lambs *must* be without blemish. The details of a perfect God are perfect! *If* God exists, *if* He is the Creator and *if* He is Infinite and Eternal, perfect in wisdom and power as well as in justice and love, it can be expected that no detail is too tiny to be put into place. God meant people to recognize the truth of truth. God means people to *understand,* and be convinced that truth is true enough to believe! He did not leave human beings with no direction as to how to find Him, how to come into communication with Him.

Isaiah goes on to say, "Yet it pleased the Lord to bruise him; he hath put him to grief: when thou shalt make his soul an offering for sin he shall see his seed, he shall prolong his days, and the pleasure of the Lord shall prosper in his hand. He shall see of the travail of his soul, and shall be satisfied: by his knowledge shall my righteous servant justify many; for he shall bear their iniquities. Therefore will I divide him a portion with the great, and he shall divide the spoil with the strong; because he hath poured out his soul unto death: and he was numbered with the transgressors; and he bare the sin of many and made intercession for the transgressors."

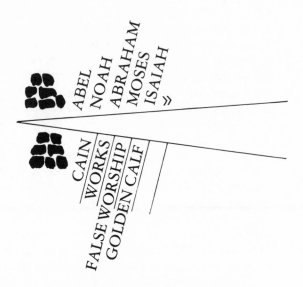

This One is indeed the promised Lamb pictured for
centuries and the time is now only seven hundred years
away! He is going to bear the sins, the iniquities, of many,
many people—people not yet born at Isaiah's time, and all who
have believed from Isaiah back! There is a "before" and "after"
in history, and God honors history. The approach on the
line of Abel to the reality of "The Lamb" is coming nearer, but
it is still seven centuries away. Not only could people know now
that this One will die for their sins, but that He will intercede
for them, that He will be a mediator, an intercessor for
transgressors. He is going to be able to do this as the High
Priest has done, but it will be different. Already the difference is
being spoken of, although not yet clearly understood. The
Shepherd of David's Psalm is to be the good Shepherd who
will come to gather His sheep in His arms as He comes to seek
and save the lost ones. The Shepherd will die for His sheep, and
to do so He will be the Lamb. The One who is the Lamb
Himself will now be able to pray for—intercede

96

NINE

for—people Himself, without bringing the blood of a lamb, because He *is* the Lamb!

Twist and turn the focus of your opera glasses, take your field glasses and get the focus right for the bird in that tree. Blurs? Indistinct? Gradually as you twist the lens with little flicks this way and that, suddenly you begin to see and you exclaim, "Oh, I see it *is* a red bird—with black tips on the wings—of course, I see it now." It is the same thing that happens as you focus your attention on the truth of what *is,* and get it out of the blur of whatever is fogging things up for you. It stands outlined against the background of blue sky, forest, and field: no illusion, this is truth. And it fits what one needs and experiences of hunger for reality in the midst of the search through the maze of lies floating abroad in murky indistinctness.

This 53rd chapter of Isaiah is as clear a focus as you can get, if you push aside the things that would blur it for you. Here is the death of the Messiah so clearly pictured that it *could* be recognized by people when it took place, and *can* be recognized as we have the prophecy and the fulfillment *both* to look back to and compare.

In the next chapter Isaiah cries out to Israel with a loud voice: "Fear not; for thou shalt not be ashamed.... For thy Maker is thine husband; the Lord of hosts is His name; and thy Redeemer the Holy One of Israel: The God of the whole earth shall he be called... For the mountains shall depart, and the hills be removed but my kindness shall not depart from thee, neither shall the covenant of my peace be removed, saith the Lord that hath mercy on thee."

What is the covenant? It is that One *is* coming who will be able to give everlasting peace, who will fulfill all the expectations through the years. God so loves His people Israel that they will not need to be ashamed. He will keep His promise to bring the Messiah, to gather them as a shepherd gathers his lambs.

In Hosea 4:1, 16 Hosea the prophet is speaking to an Israel again turned away from God, and he cries out: "Hear the word of the Lord, ye children of Israel: for the Lord hath a controversy with the inhabitants of the land, because there is *no truth,* nor *mercy,* nor *knowledge of God* in the land... For Israel slideth back as a backsliding heifer: now the Lord will feed them as a lamb in a large place."

Seven centuries later, after Jesus Christ had died, Philip, a Jewish disciple, was preaching in villages when an angel told him to go south away from Jerusalem into Gaza, the desert. Acts 8:27-35: "And he arose and went: and a man of Ethiopia, a eunuch of great authority under Candace queen of the Ethiopians, the one who had charge of all her treasure, and had come to Jerusalem for to worship, was returning, and sitting in his chariot reading Isaiah the prophet."

Imagine! Here is an Ethiopian who had worshiped in Jerusalem and he has part of the Old Testament Scripture, avidly reading it to find out the content of what God has preserved all through the centuries so that our copies read much the same as his—no significant changes—the true truth being preserved and protected through the years. Now as Philip sees this dark man eagerly reading in the chariot, the Spirit speaks to Philip and tells him why he has been led to this desert spot. "Then the Spirit said unto Philip, Go near, and join thyself to this chariot. And Philip ran thither to him and heard him read the prophet Esaias" (so you see he was reading out loud and Philip could hear where he was in the text) "and said, Do you understand what you are reading? And he said, How can I, except some man should guide me? And he asked Philip to come and sit beside him." What excitement! Here sit two men in space and time, each separated from their daily surroundings and ordinary life, reading Isaiah together in the desert. What a picture! "And the place of the scripture which he read was this, He was led as a sheep to the slaughter, and like a lamb dumb before his shearer, so opened he not his mouth: In his humiliation his judgment was taken away: and who shall declare his generation for his life is taken from the earth. And the eunuch answered Philip, and said, I pray thee, of whom speaketh the prophet this? Of himself, or of some other man?

"Then Philip opened his mouth, and began at the same Scripture, and preached unto him *Jesus*." What Philip did was to use the fifty-third chapter of Isaiah to explain to the Ethiopian the whole background of the prophecy in the Old

NINE

Testament, and what the lambs were pointing forward to, and what Isaiah was pointing forward to as he pictured the death of the Messiah. The result was that the Ethiopian went back to Ethiopia a believer that this was all true ... and that Jesus Christ was really the Messiah, the Son of God. In fact he asked Philip to baptize him before they parted from each other. We're told the eunuch went on his way rejoicing! Why not? He had found how the "pieces" fit together of the Old Testament Scripture he had, and of what had been taking place in Jerusalem in the previous few months. *Some* people did recognize Isaiah as having pictured Christ, at this time immediately after Christ's death.

TEN

The promise to Abraham was that one day all the peoples of the earth would be blessed by Someone, the Messiah, coming from the Jewish people. But before flying to the time of this One's birth, we should swoop down as a gull does ... dipping into other moments of connected history, that we might realize some more of the connections, and the continuity.

Dear young Daniel was faithful to the God of Abraham, Isaac, and Jacob. When he was only about eighteen years old he was carried off into captivity by Nebuchadnezzar along with at least three other young fellows. See these young Jews standing firm in their assurance that God is truly the living God, and that their faithfulness to Him is more important than life itself.

Do you remember the huge golden image Nebuchadnezzar had built, and the order that everyone was to bow down to it when they heard the notes of the cornet, flute, harp, sackbut, psaltery, dulcimer and other instruments? What a blast of orchestration announcing the moment of bowing! And there stand three young men upright, with some fiercely frowning at them, no doubt, and others turning pale and trembling as they imagined what would happen to them!! The penalty for not bowing was to be thrown in a burning fiery furnace. Nebuchadnezzar's question, as he announced this penalty was, "And *who* is that God that shall deliver you out of my hands?" Good question.

Three young men lifted their heads, curly brown hair, one fair with blue eyes ... we don't know, but we can imagine them, glowing with health and strength from their simple diet and exercise. They said, "We are not careful [or worried] to answer thee in this matter. If it be so, our God whom we serve is *able* to deliver us from the burning fiery furnace, and he will deliver us out of thine hand, O king. But if not, be it known unto thee, O king, that we will not serve thy gods, nor worship the golden image which thou hast set up."

The king's reaction was one of fury. He'd show them! He commanded the strongest men he had to bind the boys, and to heat the furnace seven times hotter than ever before. As the young men, dressed in their coats, hose, hats, and other garments, were thrown in, the men doing the throwing were so burned that they died. But the three bound young men fell down into the burning furnace. Now Nebuchadnezzar jumped up in haste, astonished, and said to his counselors, "Did not we cast *three* men in the furnace into the midst of the fire?" And they answered, "True, O king."

He answered and said, "Lo, I see *four* men loose, walking in the midst of the fire, and they have no hurt, and the form of the fourth is like the Son of God." Then Nebuchadnezzar came near to the mouth of the fiery burning furnace and spake, and said, "Shadrach, Meshach, and Abednego, ye servants of the most high God, come forth, and come hither." And then Shadrach, Meshach, and Abednego came forth out of the midst of the fire.

Remember this is a heathen kingdom, and these young men have been carried away here captive. The reason I am quoting the whole passage is to impress upon anyone who wants to meditate upon this factual history, the vividness of how *truth* was made known and demonstrated to these people by a few faithful Jews, that the God of Abraham is God indeed, and that their idols are nothing. Once again it is like Elijah before the priests of Baal, or David before Goliath. God has worked in answer to His children's prayer, as they have asked that men might know that He is God indeed. Do let us finish reading what came next:

"And the princes, governors, and captains, and the king's

counselors, being gathered together, *saw* these men, upon whose bodies the fire had no power, nor was an hair of their head singed, neither were their coats changed, nor the smell of fire had passed on them."

Does God care to demonstrate His existence to men? How often must He make it known? What a variety of miracles God has done, and has recorded that men through the ages might be impressed and believe. Always some believe, and many turn away, whether they are reading, or whether they are actually there to taste, smell, feel, see, and hear. These men smelled no smell of smoke, saw no scorched cloth or hair, were aware that there were no burns whether they touched them or not. It was evidence of the supernatural power of God, and they had an opportunity to compare and think about it, and come to conclusions—even as the Egyptians did! God is fair in giving series of "confrontations" which can be remembered and passed down from generation to generation.

"Then Nebuchadnezzar spake, and said, Blessed be the God of Shadrach, Meshach, and Abednego, who hath sent his angel and delivered his servants that trusted in him, and have changed the king's word, and yielded their bodies that they might not serve any God except their own God. Therefore *I make a decree,* that every people, nation, and language, which speak any thing amiss against the God of Shadrach, Meshach, and Abednego, shall be cut in pieces, and their houses shall be made a dunghill: because there is *no other God* that can deliver after this sort. Then the king promoted the three young men in the province of Babylon."

This was a pretty big turn-about! First the king throws them in the furnace because they won't bow to the idol, and then he is so overwhelmingly convinced by the miracle of God's working that he orders everyone to be cut up in little pieces if they say anything against the *God* of Shadrach, Meshach, and Abednego!! You see the faithfulness of the men drew attention not to themselves, but to the living God in whom they believed, and whom they trusted so implicitly. Yes, faithful Jews were a blessing to the Gentile people among whom they lived, just as the unfaithful ones affected their own children by turning away to false gods—jumping down to Cain's line, in other words.

Daniel's own time in the lion's den as an old man was another time of proof to the kingdom that the God of Daniel was God indeed. Amazingly, Daniel—right there in his captivity—was given visions and understanding of future events into the time of the great tribulation, and the second coming of Christ, so that his contribution along with others whom God chose to write the Bible was to help complete all that God would have people throughout history, and us ourselves, know ... as we now wait for the *next* step. People made a melange, or mixture, of future events so that Jews expected a king and a kingdom and skipped over the expectation of a *Lamb* who would die as the final atonement, to do away with the need of the lambs dying as "pictures" of the atonement. The prophecies concerning the second coming of the Messiah were sometimes given in such a way that people could not distinguish that there would be so many years between the two events.

Sometimes when we get very near something, we can't see it properly at all. Every farsighted person experiences this in trying to read without glasses—all becomes a blur. True of faces, too, for some of us! Think how some oil paintings look if you get too close to them, if they were painted for a more distant view! The distance from which we are looking often affects the perspective we get. To be able to read a *fair* history book gives one a more clear idea of what really took place, than to read the newspapers of the period one is reading about. But of course the history book has to be fair. Now the Bible is *God's* portrayal of history, science (where it touches on science), true doctrine as to sin and what to do about it in order to be forgiven, and events coming in the future. If God has given men the knowledge supernaturally as to what to write about events before they were born, or that which will come after they die, then it is accurate.

This does not mean the writers of the Old Testament understood every detail they themselves wrote. There is a verse in the New Testament which says that now we see

TEN

through a glass, darkly, but one day we will see with crystal clarity!

However, seeing through a glass darkly *is still seeing something.* Isaiah wrote a very clear description of the Lamb being judged unfairly, and dying for His people as a substitute. Daniel wrote of the Messiah coming as king. Both were right. The Messiah was to be both things—but the time was to be separated, and people got mixed up. At the time the Messiah came a lot of the Jews got mixed up, but *some didn't.*

There is one passage in Isaiah which refers first to the first coming of the Messiah, and then to the second coming. Jesus read this passage out loud in the Synagogue. You find that in Luke 4:15-20. It was in Nazareth where He had been brought up, and as He did every Sabbath day He went in to the Synagogue on the Sabbath day and stood up to read. "And there was given him the book of the prophet Isaiah (Esaias). And when he had opened the book, he found the place where it was written, The Spirit of the Lord is upon me, because he hath anointed me to preach the gospel to the poor; he hath sent me to heal the brokenhearted, to preach deliverance to the captives, and recovering of sight to the blind, to set at liberty them that are bruised, to preach the acceptable year of the Lord. And he closed the book, and gave it again to the minister, and sat down. And the eyes of all who were in the synagogue were upon him. And he began to say to them, This day is this scripture fulfilled in your ears."

If you turn to Isaiah 61 and read that passage, you will see that it goes on to say that there will be a day of vengeance of our God, and that there will be comfort given those who mourn in Zion, and that they will be given beauty for ashes and the oil of joy for mourning. It goes on to speak of that which will be taking place at the second coming of the Messiah. You see Jesus made it very clear for any who would really have listened, or for us if we listen now. He declared that *that* day the portion He read was fulfilled. He had come as the Messiah to fulfill the first portion, and He tells later that He is coming back again. Then the second portion will be fulfilled.

However, this is going on into what we will look at later. First we need to fly to another two moments of history, or places of writing, in the Old Testament to continue the continuity.

Yes, these are not isolated bits and pieces—amusing fantasies, timely little parables, myths and fables—but history, doctrine, prophecy of the future. Here we have the explanation of what man needs to *know* to find the solution to his basic questions—his search: search for truth, search for God, search for a meaning to life—this is what God gave to man in the Bible: *answers!* How horrible it would be if *man* had to judge as to what *in* the Bible *might* turn out to be the word of God, and what might simply be the mishmash of man's writing. What a trap to be placed in, if God surrounded His word with a maze of paths leading to a dead end, and we needed to follow one maze path after another to try to find the "way out into truth." This is one of Satan's subtle lies to the intelligence. Our God is honest in His dealings with men through all the ages, and He has not covered up His true word, but has kept it intact and has had it translated into many languages so that men *could* have His communication to them. Century after century men are cruel to the next generation in muddying up what God has made clear. Don't get caught in the form of that which is taking place in this generation, for yourself, or for your children. Get it straightened out as to the reality of the fact that men are creatures created by the Creator, and that God speaks in judgment of men, but that man is not equipped with infinite knowledge and understanding, so is in a very poor position to judge God's message, or to "edit" His Book. Remember that Satan was the first to "edit" God's Word when he changed it for Eve.

Our bird flight has been circling, but now we dip down to continue the view of God's unchanging way to Himself, as it unfolds. Always His perfect holiness and justice is balanced by His perfect love and compassion.

In Deuteronomy 4, God is speaking to Israel about keeping His laws and continuing in the worship as He has set it forth, *not forgetting* what has been seen, or handed down to them. Verse 9: "Only take heed to thyself and keep thy soul diligently, lest thou forget the things which thine eyes have

TEN

seen, and lest they depart from thy heart all the days of thy life: but teach them thy sons, and thy sons' sons." God goes on to warn that if generation after generation goes away from the true worship, and does evil in the sight of God, He will scatter them among all the nations, and each group will be few in number among the nations into which they have been scattered. But then follows a deep call and promise from the loving God who longs to have His people in close communication with Himself. Verse 29: "But *if* from thence thou shalt *seek* the Lord thy God, thou shalt find Him, if thou seek him with all thy heart and with all thy soul."

And in Deuteronomy 30:1-3, 10: "And it shall come to pass, when all these things are come upon thee, the blessing and the curse which I have set before thee, and thou shalt call them to mind among all the nations, whither the Lord thy God hath driven thee, and shalt *return unto the Lord thy God,* and shalt obey his voice according to all that I command thee this day, thou and thy children, with all thine heart, and with all thy soul; That *then* the Lord thy God will turn thy captivity, and have compassion upon thee, and will return and gather thee from all nations whither the Lord thy God hath scattered thee... If thou shalt hearken unto the voice of the Lord thy God to keep his commandments and his statutes which are written in this book of the law, and if thou turn unto the Lord thy God with all thine heart and with all thy soul."

And in Nehemiah 1:8, 9: "Remember, I beseech thee, the word that thou commandedst thy servant Moses, saying, If ye transgress, I will scatter you abroad among the nations: But if ye turn unto me and keep my commandments, and do them; though there were of you cast out unto the uttermost part of the heaven, yet will I gather them from thence, and I will bring them unto the place that I have chosen to set my name there. Now these are thy servants and thy people, whom thou hast redeemed by thy great power and by thy strong hand."

Nehemiah is praying, calling out to God to remember His promise to His people. He is praying that God will help the people at *that* time to again have their place. The rebuilding of the wall under Nehemiah, with the king giving help, and with the people gathering to build, brought a blast of contempt from Sanballat: "What do these feeble Jews? ..." laughing at their attempt to make a comeback. Nehemiah answers with believing prayer again, asking God to help. However, he also led the people in building, and in standing watch ready to fight, and for the duration of the work no one took off his clothing except to wash it, as they worked day and night in shifts, guarding the walls and laboring to build. God heard and answered Nehemiah's prayer at that time.

How marvelously the Jews have been preserved through the centuries! No other nation has had such a history. They have not been absorbed into the nations where they have been scattered. Why? Because they are a "people" chosen in Abraham, and a promise has been given which will be finally brought to conclusion in future times. The Jews, as Jews, will continue to be a people. It is one of the supernatural proofs of the truth of the Word of God. And so they march before our eyes as we "fly" over the past: Jacob, Joseph, Moses, Joshua, Samuel, David, Solomon, Elijah, Elisha, Ezra, Nehemiah—*always* a remnant in every period, and always *some* who believed, and *some* who handed down the truth to the next generation. But thank God He chose among them the ones to whom He was going to give inspiration to write His account of it all. Thank God we have a true, consecutive picture, and the clear emphasis on *how* to come to God, and what that means practically in our own moment of history. Thank God He is able to preserve His message and to have given it so that it is timely and fresh for today's needs—for Jews, and for anyone else who cares to read.

2 Chronicles 15:2-4 speaks again of the need of "reality" in the area of seeking and being honest in the search for truth and for the true God. "The Lord is with you while ye be found with him; and if ye seek him, he will be found of you; but if ye forsake him, he will forsake you. Now for a long season Israel hath been without the true God, and without a teaching priest, and without law. But when they in their trouble did turn unto the Lord God of Israel, and sought him, he was found of them."

TEN

People often talk of their desire for "reality" in the area of wanting to know God exists, but they don't seem to consider that the Personal God has asked for a "reality" of man's sincerity and honesty in search for Him. Jeremiah makes this clear in 29:11-13: "For I know the thoughts that I think toward you, saith the Lord, thoughts of peace, and not of evil, to give you an expected end. Then shall ye call upon me, and ye shall go and pray unto me, and I will hearken unto you. And ye shall seek me, and find me, when ye shall search for me with all your heart."

To hear a man's or woman's voice sing Handel's solo, "If with all your heart ye truly seek me, ye shall ever surely find me," beats through one's chest with some sort of a throb depending on how well he or she is singing, and how much you respond to this kind of music. But no matter how much you may "enjoy" Handel's solo, the words are not meant to be entertainment! This is God's promise to human beings from the time of Adam and Eve: If your search is honest, sincere, with a desire to know God (if He exists) and to bow before Him (if He is there) in the way which He sets forth to you, so that you may become one of His people, *then* the promise is to you. If all you have is a curiosity, or a shallow interest, with no desire ever to bow but only a determination to keep your free, "bloody but unbowed head" from inclining, then the promise has nothing to do with you. The condition is one of wholeheartedness or honest sincerity of desiring to *know* so that the result will be one of coming into a relationship that is lasting.

Isaiah says in this same direction, in 55:6, 7: "Seek ye the Lord while he may be found, call ye upon him while he is near. Let the wicked forsake his way, and the unrighteous man his thoughts: and let him return unto the Lord, and he will have mercy upon him; and to our God, for he will abundantly pardon."

He will *abundantly* pardon? On what basis? Does one have to *keep* the law? Well, if it were on the basis of the law, the ten commandments, and the deeper areas of what is going on inside our minds and emotions, attitudes, and reactions where men can't see them—if it is to be on the basis of *doing* and *being* what would fit in with the requirements of our own standards, let alone God's standards—what chance would any one of us have for being "abundantly pardoned" and returned to a place of communication with the God of the ages?

Then, you see, we follow the line of the Lamb all the way from Abel, Noah, Abraham, Moses, David, and come to stand (in our imaginations) beside the High Priest in the holy of holies to see that the lid of the mercy seat fits perfectly—no cracks! It covers the law, and when the blood of the lamb is sprinkled upon it on the Day of Atonement, the significance is that for each one who comes believing the law has been covered by the blood of the lamb. The High Priest represents the whole congregation. Coming back to God, in the days of Jeremiah, Nehemiah, Isaiah, meant coming back to the close relationship which was entered into with God on the basis of worshiping Him in the manner He had given, *not* coming with a list of good works. One could *not* ever *buy* one's way into His presence with any kind of payment—of moral good works or religious good works or huge amounts of material gifts. Everyone needed to come with a reality of something going on *inside* himself or herself. The way was open to those who were honest and sincere in the areas where only God could see the reality. Belief in the truth of what God made clear in His spoken word, or written Word, has been, since the beginning, the necessary ingredient. "Faith" as a mystical kind of fog, descending upon some fortunate people, but not on others, is *not* what the word of God has ever taught. God's own statement about this is, "Faith cometh by hearing, and hearing cometh by the word of God." You have to hear something you can think about in your mind and conclude to be true, in order to believe it.

Before we leave the Old Testament, come to the first of the minor prophets, Jonah. Jonah is mentioned in the book of Kings (2 Kings 14:25), so we can place him historically. However the short book about his experience in Nineveh is important in understanding that this promise of God, "If with all your heart you truly seek me, you shall surely find me," applies not just to Jews.

TEN

How can we know that anyone in the wicked city of Nineveh was truly seeking God? I think it is clear from the way God sent His words and warning to that place, so that they could *hear* the word of God, and have the opportunity to believe. It seems to me the results help us to understand that the compassion of God is demonstrated in the reality of His making it possible for the sincerely seeking hearts to find Him.

It's too bad that so much controversy about the possibility of a great fish being able to swallow a man has made Jonah, the very book where the compassion of God is so clearly demonstrated for all centuries to look back upon, one which people can't "see" clearly because of the dust in their eyes! Satan cleverly attacks the very places where the central truth is being unfolded, like the early parts of Genesis (Creation and the Fall), without which no one can understand what follows. What is the sense of redemption, if there was no fall! So with Jonah; if all the discussion is drawn off away from what really was going on, people simply smile or sneer and feel superior and miss the basic truth. Mission accomplished! That is what Satan wanted.

Jonah, a Jew, a prophet of Israel, one of the tribe of Zebulun, son of Amittai, receives the word of the Lord—a verbalized, spoken, understandable command, saying: "Arise, go to Nineveh, that great city, and cry against it; for their wickedness is come up before me."

Jonah's reaction to the command of God was not very commendable for a prophet. He went—in the opposite direction as fast as he could go. He didn't want to go to a whole goy city, an uncircumcised people, and tell them anything. He was so rebellious at the idea that he wanted to get away from the place where the Lord had spoken to him, so we are told he tried to flee from the presence of the Lord by going to a seaport, Joppa, and taking a ship that was going to Tarshish. He paid his fare, got into the ship, and happily felt he had succeeded in getting away from the Lord and his unwanted commission.

Jonah 1:4: "But the Lord sent out a great wind into the sea, and there was a mighty tempest in the sea, so that the ship was like to be broken."

This really frightened the sailors and every one of them cried out to his own god, and also threw overboard everything they could think of so that the ship would be lighter. But Jonah was blissfully asleep below, unaware of the uproar on deck. The shipmaster sought him out, asking, in verse 6, "What meanest thou, O sleeper? arise, call upon thy God, if so be that God will think upon us that we perish not."

Now the sailors said at this point, "Let's cast lots, and whoever the lot falls on, we'll know that one is the cause of this evil falling upon us all." So they did exactly that, and the lot fell upon Jonah. Now they asked him, "Tell us for what reason all this is happening. What is your occupation? Where do you come from? What is your country, of what people are you?"

Now we must say for Jonah that at this point he was excruciatingly honest, and in no way tried to hide the truth. At this point he really stood up and spoke for the true and living God and declared His existence as he said, "I am an Hebrew; I fear the Lord, the God of heaven, which has made the sea and the dry land." Now he speaks of the One true God who is the Creator, without any attempt to compromise. He also went on to tell them that he had run away from this God, and that he was sure that was the reason for the storm, in which their lives were in danger as well as his own. We know this from the next verse in which we are told: "Then were the men exceedingly afraid, and said unto him, Why hast thou done this? For the men knew he had fled from the presence of the Lord, because he had told them."

Their next question was, "What shall we do unto thee that the sea may be calm unto us?" And Jonah replied with courage, ready to take what he felt he deserved that the others might not go down with him, "Take me up and cast me forth into the sea; so shall the sea be calm unto you, for I know that for my sake this great tempest is upon you."

The men really were very concerned about Jonah at that point. They must have been attracted by his honesty and courage. They tried to row very hard to bring the ship to land, but it was impossible. So they called out—not to their gods now, but to the Lord of Jonah—asking Him to not allow them to die for

TEN

this man's sake, but to save their lives. After this prayer they took Jonah and cast him overboard, and he disappeared from their sight, and immediately the storm stopped. What a proof to these men that the God of Jonah was God indeed. It would seem to me that some or all of these men were honest in their search for truth, because we are told that they feared the Lord exceedingly, and offered a sacrifice to the Lord and made vows. This certainly was a different reaction than Pharaoh had in Egypt when he saw miracles. People don't automatically believe when they hear of, or see, the results of someone's prayer and God's answering that prayer.

Now we are told that the Lord had *prepared* a great fish to swallow up Jonah. Great fish have swallowed men, and the men have come through the experience alive, but this one was especially prepared to be in the right place at the right time, so that Jonah would not drown. God was keeping Jonah alive to do what He had for him to do in his moment of history, and was giving him another opportunity to do it.

Picture Jonah in the belly of the fish. Uncomfortable indeed, but now praying with all his might. He is not just screaming, "Help!" but he is aware of the wonder of being still in communication with the living God, even at the bottom of the sea. His prayer is a marvelous piece of understanding prose, expressing the reality of a life caught in the middle of desperate depression. Jonah was at "the bottom" literally, but many people could identify with his feelings as they are "at the bottom" psychologically, emotionally, spiritually, agonizing as to what life might be all about. Listen to his words in chapter 2: "I cried by reason of mine affliction unto the Lord, and he heard me; out of the belly of hell cried I, and thou heardest my voice... The floods compassed me about: all thy billows and thy waves passed over me. Then I said, I am cast out of thy sight; yet I will look again toward thy holy temple. The waters compassed me about, even to the soul: the depth closed me round about, the weeds were wrapped about my head. I went down to the bottoms of the mountains; the earth with her bars was about me for ever: yet hast thou brought up my life from corruption, O Lord my God. When my soul fainted within me, then remembered I the Lord: and my prayer came in unto thee, into thine holy temple ... I will sacrifice unto thee with the voice of thanksgiving; I will pay that I have vowed. Salvation is of the Lord."

This is the prayer of a man who believes God. It is the prayer of a man who trusts the promises of God, and who knows he will be forgiven, on the basis of true sacrifice. He has hope. He knows he has much of which to be forgiven, but he calls out on the basis of the promises and understanding he has had.

The great fish vomits Jonah on the dry land, safe in the land of the living now, but there is something beyond this. Jonah has come back to the God who has "abundantly pardoned" him, even as Isaiah taught He would!

When Jonah was once more asked by the Lord to "arise and go unto Nineveh, that great city, and preach unto it the preaching that I bid thee," he went! It took him three days to get there, but he went, and he did start preaching a warning, that within forty days Nineveh would be overthrown.

Please remember that Noah preached this same kind of a message to the world at his time. Also that Lot told the people of Sodom and Gomorrah this kind of a message. No one except Noah's family came into the ark for safety, and not even all of Lot's family came out with him. People simply don't believe God's word just because it is an alarming warning. The reaction of many *many* through history has been to laugh and continue in whatever they are doing. Prophecy of the future tells us that it will be like this when Jesus comes back again. In spite of the completeness of the information the whole Bible gives men now, the majority are not believing it, and accepting God's "abundant pardon" in preparation for the rest of eternity. We are told that it will be "like the days of Sodom and Gomorrah" in the time approaching the "end." People will be marrying and having children, entertaining themselves and dying, having wars and rumors of more wars—and always there will be the optimists basing their predictions of utopia on no base at all!

Nineveh was a city with a king who certainly must have been seeking in some measure to know the truth, ready to believe the

114

message of the true and living God if only he could hear it. Jonah preached to a receptive, prepared group of people—ones who illustrate the reality of that promise "if with all thine heart you truly seek me, you shall surely find me." One might add, "Even if my prophet, my servant, runs off in the other direction, I will turn him back to the place where he will go to talk to you." So many times this has taken place in history since Jonah's time, when people, ministers or doctors, farmers or fishermen, against their own "wills" or "plans" have been "sent" to a place, a person, a country, a group of people, and have found that the person, country, group have been "prepared." It is a mystery to the finite, limited minds what the difference is, but God tells us it is the great difference between honest, wholehearted seeking and indifference.

When Jonah preached, the people of Nineveh believed God, and proclaimed a fast and put on sackcloth to show repentance for their sins. When word came to the king as to what was being preached, the king got up and put off his royal robes and put on sackcloth and sat in ashes, humbly proclaiming that he was sorry for his sin and the sin of the whole city. He called a complete fasting time for everyone. A tremendous picture of the blessing of the Jewish prophet's giving the message of the living God to a heathen nation! The flow of history was changed for this people: God did not destroy them, and they not only repented but "turned away from the violence they had done," in other words, they *really* changed, showing outwardly the reality of what had taken place inwardly.

Jonah, however, wasn't happy! In fact, he was very angry and told God he knew he was a gracious God, and would be merciful and not punish the people in the end, and that is why he ran away into Tarshish in the first place! Jonah would have preferred the city to be destroyed, and ended with a plea to die, saying that now that these people had been spared, he'd rather die! God gives Jonah an object lesson by causing a supernaturally fast growing gourd to grow up over a shelter to give Jonah a coolness as he sat in the midday sun. Then as Jonah sat watching the city in his disgruntled state, he appreciated the cool shade. A worm came along, prepared by God to attack the gourd plant the next morning, and it withered, so that Jonah fainted with the blast of heat that day, and cried out again to die. Now it is to Jonah that God speaks, showing to him, and to us, the definiteness of His compassion to mankind. He says, "You, Jonah, have pity on a gourd plant's withering and dying? Should I not then spare Nineveh, where there are more than 120,000 people who can't tell the difference between their right and left hands, plus many cattle?"

What is the difference between these people, and the people who are not Jews, in *other* moments of Old Testament history, and the people who are today not believers in the living God? It seems that these were inwardly "seeking" so that when they *heard* the truth, they believed God.

Isaiah says to us as a message from God in 55:11: "So shall my word be that goeth forth out of my mouth: it shall not return to me void, but it shall accomplish that which I please, and it shall prosper in the thing whereto I sent it."

Where there are seeking hearts, God's word will be as seed planted in a fertile ground! This fact does not change. Nor does His Word change.

You are hearing today!!

ELEVEN

If we have identified throughout this flight through history with the ones believing that God is speaking truth which is understandable, we will come with breathless awe, as I imagine the angels did, to the moment when the brief years to divide history and time so sharply, began. The important moment so long waited for, so long looked forward to, so long expected in faith, so long ago promised to Eve, arrived with the beginning of a pregnancy. A unique virgin pregnancy! A lovely young girl, pregnant.

A virgin pregnant? Impossible! How could it be? Anyone knows a man's sperm is involved in any pregnancy. Whether women like it or not, a man's sperm is involved in the making of a new person. Whether men like it or not, a woman's seed is also involved, as is the womb where the new human being takes its nine months of time to grow. A virgin birth—impossible? No, *unique*.

How can a thing be totally *unique* if it has ever happened before? If someone tries to sell you a "unique original" art object of which no copies are in existence, and another one is purchased by your friend in another city, you cry out, "I've been gypped ... it's a fake!" A really unique thing is a one and only, even though the word may be carelessly used to just mean "special." God spoke to the serpent and said way back there that the seed of a woman would bruise his head. The promise was given that someone, the Messiah, would be born of a

woman. That woman would come through the line of
Abraham, David, Solomon, and so on, but there was to be
something very special about his birth. Isaiah, in chapter 7:14,
prophesies: "Therefore the Lord himself shall give you a *sign;*
Behold a virgin shall conceive, and bear a son, and shall call his
name Immanuel." God cared about making things clear, and
God's signs are clear. If you crash when you go through a red
light, or because you haven't bothered to notice road signs that
have been clearly posted, no officer is going to give you much
sympathy. The signs God has given so that people can
recognize the truth are clear, but it is necessary to *look* in order
to see them.

Yes, a virgin birth was to be one of the *signs* that the one
born was the Messiah. As this was to be Immanuel, or God
with us, the one who had always lived, the Second Person of
the Trinity, the birth of this One had to be different. This was
God the Son, coming down to become truly Man so that he
could take man's place, be the substitute and die for man.
He had to have a different birth; anything *else* would be
impossible, rather than the virgin birth being impossible. Now
the Jews had *expected* and looked forward to the fact that the
Messiah would be born to some girl, and every generation
of believing Jews would have talked about it as a rather
awesome possibility in their own time, even as believers in the
Bible as God's Word today, feel awesome about the possibility
of the Messiah coming back in our time.

However, now that the moment had arrived and day-by-day
life was no different than before, there were people who needed a
very special preparation for that immediate moment. Mary and
Joseph each needed reassurance, and Mary needed another
woman to talk to who would be prepared to believe her story.
God, who is a gentle, understanding heavenly Father, gave what
was needed to these Jews who were being given a task which
could have been run from very easily!

The preparation began with the answer to prayer given to
the priest Zacharias and his wife Elizabeth, who was a daughter of
Aaron. Elizabeth was old, too old to have children, and an
angel appeared to Zacharias while he was burning incense in

ELEVEN

the temple, and told him his wife would have a son. Now,
having an angel talk to you ought to be convincing, but Zacharias
asked for a sign that this was true, and he was struck dumb,
unable to speak for the nine months of pregnancy, as a sign!
All this would, you may be sure, be very impressive to
Zacharias, and to Elizabeth. They were prepared to believe Mary
when she came to them with her story of what an angel had said
to *her,* and as Elizabeth was Mary's cousin, she was the very one
to whom she would naturally run, expecially as Mary would
be told about her cousin's miraculous pregnancy in her old age.

God sent an angel to speak to Mary, to tell her she had
been chosen by God to conceive in her womb and bring forth a
son whose name should be Jesus. "He shall be great, and shall be
called the son of the Highest: and the Lord God shall give unto
him the throne of his father David: and he shall reign over
the house of Jacob forever: and of his kingdom there shall be
no end."

Clear? This is no ordinary man, this is the Messiah. Two lines
of promises have been made about Him in the Old
Testament: He will suffer for His people, He will stand as a
sheep before shearers is dumb, He will be the Lamb; but also He
is to be King with a Kingdom that will never end! This One
promised to Mary as her Son is to be the Messiah; his birth
has to be unique in all history; it *can* only take place once. Of
course there is no precedent. Now Mary was an ordinary Jewish
girl, in that she was no different in birth from anyone else. She
was obviously a faithful, believing Jew, believing God's
word up to the level of her understanding, and what happened
in the next few minutes proved that she was ready to believe all
that God made clear to her through the angel. Her question
was down to earth and honest. "How shall this be, seeing I
know not a man?" How can I have a child when I have been
chaste and virgin in waiting for my marriage to Joseph? It is
impossible. This was her expressed feeling, but she was not
scoffing, she was asking an *honest* question. There is a lot of
difference between asking a trick question with intent to trip
up a person, and asking an honest question waiting for
information.

When the angel explained that something very special would take place, that the Holy Spirit, the third person of the Trinity, would overshadow her with supernatural power to cause this to take place, Mary believed. You see, the angel took time to continue his explanation with special detail, somewhat like this. Mary, this seems impossible to you, but you see, with God nothing is impossible. Your cousin Elizabeth is in the sixth month of a pregnancy in her old age, and she has been barren all her married life. Yes, Mary was given an honest, careful answer—but the special thing is, she *believed* it to be true, and was willing to "bow" before God, accepting the task.

The help of having another human being to talk to—two of them, in fact—who were prepared to believe her and discuss the wonder of it all, was such an understanding kindness on the part of Mary's heavenly Father, and ours. Mary ran off to visit Elizabeth and Zacharias. Mary was full of her story you can imagine, and eager to tell someone who would not scoff. But God gave an additional "sign" to Mary, because Elizabeth was the one who began the conversation with a greeting in a loud voice, saying, "You are blessed among women, Mary, blessed is the fruit of your womb. How is it that the mother of my Lord should come to me? As soon as you greeted me, Mary, my baby leapt in my womb for joy. Blessed are you, Mary, for believing, because there will be a performance of those things which were told you from the Lord." You see God gave Elizabeth both special knowledge by revelation, and understanding. There had been a kind of leap different from the usual kicking of her baby which alerted her, and she must have been given revelation as to what was taking place in Mary. Also Elizabeth had been prepared by the fact that Zacharias had told her (in writing, as he could not yet speak) that an angel had spoken to him, so for six months her thoughts had revolved about the supernatural. Being the wife of a priest and a believer, it is certain that Elizabeth would have been very familiar with Isaiah. Do you think the fourteenth verse of the seventh chapter was known to her? It is sure to have been.

Elizabeth was the first human being who *knowingly* beheld the virgin whom Isaiah had promised seven centuries

ELEVEN

before. Elizabeth beheld a virgin who had conceived, and it was her cousin. What a moment for Elizabeth! Here stand two Jewish women, an old one—barren for so many years of having "known a man," her husband the priest—now pregnant, and a very young one—believing and chaste, waiting for marriage to the man she loved—with a life commencing in her whom the older one had already acknowledged as "my Lord." How far can you get from a mystical, other-worldly, impossible-to-put-into-language, kind of religion? This is history, on this earth, involving very human human beings, fulfilling years of past promises, giving forth tangible proof.

People act as if Christianity is a new religion which just sprang up two thousand years ago, but it is not new, it is simply a continuation. It is a fulfillment. It is a next step. It is the proof that the covenant with Abraham was true. It is Jewish. It goes back to the promise given after Adam and Eve fell—the seed of a woman will bruise the head of the serpent—and it turned out to be Mary's seed. Elizabeth's little cousin Mary was the person being talked about all those centuries before, and the Infinite, Personal God *knew* it was going to be Mary. But He did not treat her like a computer into which He was putting a card; she was given choice. Her question was answered, and her moment of choice was real, after which she answered, "Behold the handmaid of the Lord, be it unto me according to thy word." Mary bowed, the creature before the Creator, and said, "I am willing to do your will."

Joseph also needed reassurance. He loved Mary but he was confused by what had happened. It was then that the angel of the Lord appeared to Joseph in a dream to help him take literally what Mary had told him. It was harder for Joseph to take the virgin birth as literally true than anyone else who has ever lived, because he was emotionally involved in the very evident fact of Mary's pregnancy, and knew he had nothing to do with it. The angel says, "Joseph, thou son of David," (to make things detail perfect in this respect, not only was Mary of the line of David, but Joseph, who would be head of the family into which Jesus was being born, also came of the line of David) "fear not to take unto thee Mary thy wife: for that which is conceived in her is of the Holy Ghost. And she shall bring forth a son, and thou shalt call his name Jesus: for he shall save his people from their sins."

Joseph is told that which ties up this virgin-born child with the promised suffering Messiah who will save His people from their sins. Then Matthew goes on to say in chapter 1:22, 23, so we will have no doubt about it being the fulfillment: "Now all this was done, that it might be fulfilled which was spoken of the Lord by the prophet, saying, Behold a virgin shall be with child and shall bring forth a son, and they shall call his name Emmanuel, which being interpreted is, God with us. Then Joseph being raised from sleep did as the angel of the Lord had bidden him, and took unto him his wife: And knew her not till she had brought forth her firstborn son, and he called his name Jesus."

Yes, Joseph was convinced. He took Mary to protect and care for her during the months ahead, convinced that his home was to be the home into which the promised Messiah, whom Isaiah and other prophets had spoken of, would be born. He waited until after that birth had taken place, to become physically one with Mary, so that the Messiah indeed was not only conceived in a virgin supernaturally, but was actually born of a virgin, so that the *sign* was literal, and recognizable.

One wonders, when Mary and Joseph set forth at the time of the payment of taxes, whether they remembered the verse in the minor prophet Micah, 5:2, which so clearly set forth the place of the Messiah's birth. It too had been written about 700 years before, and was available Scripture for Jews to read. It would seem likely that the priest Zacharias knew it well as a portion of Scripture, but did it dawn upon him until *after* the birth? It would be very human of him *not* to think of it until later, in spite of the clarity: "But thou, Bethlehem Ephratah, though thou be little among the thousands of Judah, yet out of thee shall *he* come forth unto me that is to be ruler in Israel; whose goings forth have been from of old, from everlasting." Who sings, using this word "everlasting" over and over again, so familiar to the Jews? Even David in his psalms, such as Psalm 90:1, 2: "Lord, thou hast been our dwelling place in all generations. Before the mountains were brought forth, or ever thou hadst formed the earth and the world, even from everlasting to everlasting thou art God."

The writers of the four Gospels presented the birth and life of the Messiah with four different emphases. Matthew was written especially to the Jews, giving the genealogies to start with, that the Messiah might be shown to be of the right lineage. Mark wrote to show that Jesus came as a servant to minister to man, and begins with His ministry, and that of John the Baptist preparing the way. Luke wrote from a physician's viewpoint especially stressing the humanity of Jesus. And John, who writes to tell the things which show clearly that Jesus really is God, the Messiah who is from everlasting, reduces the whole birth to this emphatic sentence: "In the beginning was the Word, and the Word was with God, and the Word was God. The same was in the beginning with God. All things were made by him; and without him was not anything made that was made." John is presenting sharply and decisively that this Messiah has always existed, was there before creation, in fact that nothing that was made was made without Him.

Murky dark, filled with smoked perfume is not the atmosphere of what is being given in God's Word. Sunshine in the Swiss Alps, with air unspoiled by pollution, portrays more the kind of searchlight this true truth can take. God has made things clear, and men have muddied it up with their own doubting explanations. Doubt like a smog fills men's pompous gobbledegook religious statements. Add that to the unbelievers' scissors which cut the rest of it away, and what do you have left?

There is the statement God has given us through the Messiah, "If a son asks for bread, will his father give him stones?" The answer is clear: no, a good father will give bread that can be digested. Had unbelieving liberal theologians dropped the manna, the rattle of pebbles would have been like hail—frighteningly unfulfilling, yes, even killing the children who would have rushed out openmouthed! No, the same God who sent manna to fulfill the physical need for bread has sent the spiritual manna, the Bread of Life, at the exact, perfect moment in history, to fill the need of those who had looked

forward to Him. Their expectation was not in vain. And we who
examine the evidence with really open minds and honest,
seeking hearts, need not be disappointed or ashamed. What
we will find is true truth, which is a power to those who believe,
in any period of history.

Where will this Messiah, the Son of God, the Everlasting
One, Prince of Peace, Lord of lords, be born? In some
majestic place fitting such a One? In some place reminiscent of
the glory in heaven? Is it a *mistake* that the inns were crowded,
that Mary and Joseph that night could find no "suitable" place
for *any* human birth, let alone the birth of such a One?

No, no mistake when you have followed the lamb
throughout the Old Testament as we have just done. Where else
would a lamb be born than in a stable? And so the picture
became perfect: this one who was to be the great Shepherd
of all the sheep of His fold, this one who was going to lay down
His life for His sheep, had come to be the *Lamb,* the long
expected Lamb, who indeed would be the atonement. What a
perfect place for the detail-perfect God to choose for the
birth of the Lamb!

But go one step further in the beauty of this picture. To whom
was the birth of the lamb first announced? To shepherds
keeping their flock by night! Who more suitable to first
come to *see* the Lamb! How amazing that the Great Shepherd
who had come to die for His lambs, and needed to become a Lamb
to do it, was announced to the *shepherds* on the hills who were
among the ones for whom He would die. The lambs come to
look at their substitute! The lambs who were shepherds *and*
lambs at the same time came to look at the Lamb of God, who
would also be their Shepherd and who would die for them.

Could they possibly know all this, these lowly shepherds
keeping their flocks on those hills? They were Jews. They
surely knew something of Abraham's sacrifice of Isaac and the
ram caught in the thickets. They surely knew something of the
Passover looking back to Moses' lambs, and the blood on
the doorposts before leaving Egypt. They surely knew
something of Isaiah and his prophecies. Maybe even one of them
excitedly remembered that verse tucked away there in Micah,

ELEVEN

about Bethlehem being an important spot. Anyway,
whatever they recounted to each other on that hasty trip down
the hillside, their ears were ringing with the angel's message:
"Behold, I bring you good tidings of great joy, which shall be to
all people ..." Oh, Abraham, are you listening? Here it is!
The covenant is about to be fulfilled! Your seed—a blessing to
all people.

"For unto you is born this day in the city of David, a Savior,
which is Christ the Lord." Clear? Yes, the shepherds had a
clear message, and they believed it, and acted on that belief.
They ran down the hill in response. Was it a "spiritual
happening?" If you mean they did not stumble and get bruised
toes, if you mean they did not sweat, or have an accelerated
heartbeat, if you mean they did not get in each other's way and
get irritated, *no*, it was not a spiritual happening. It was an historic
happening which was titanic in importance; it was happening in
space and time and it took minutes to get down the hill, and
the ground was as uneven and full of rocks as it ever had been.
Bethlehem was still Bethlehem, and the stable was as smelly of
manure as it ever had been.

A "sign" had been given them, that they might have no
difficulty being sure. Is God pleased to answer our
questions ...? Intellectual, spiritual, psychological, emotional—
are questions barred? The Word of God gives all we need to
know, and then, we need to *believe* what has been said by God.

The shepherds were looking for a stable with a newborn
baby in it, wrapped in swaddling clothes. The angels had
disappeared. The music of the song was still echoing in their ears:
"Glory to God in the highest," but it could not be turned on for
a replay; it was finished, and the sky was dark again, the
night air was silent. They had to *believe* what they *had* heard,
and act on it. And when they approached the stable, that baby
which after all was like any other newborn Jewish baby, was in
his first moment of having "no form or comeliness that we
should desire Him." Isaiah had prophesied that He would *not*
be different nor even particularly beautiful or desirable as far as
human looks went, and here are the first moments of that being
a fact.

But the shepherds believed what the angels had told them. Perhaps you say, "They had sufficient reason to believe." Oh, but not as much reason as we have to believe. They were standing in an old familiar stable, and seeing a sight they had seen often before, a baby with a mother and one who seemed to be the father. But they did two things as a result: they went around *telling* other people what the angels had said, and what they had found, *and* they glorified God and praised Him for all they had heard and seen. So they believed, and thanked God.

They didn't go back to the hillside and their sheep with a mystical Experience which could not be verbalized. They went back with plenty to talk about to each other, in fact, so much to talk about that they had gone from friend to friend to tell, in human language, the things which Luke says in chapter 2:18: "And all they that heard it wondered at these things which were *told* them by the shepherds." These were facts which they could believe to be true, or not—factual, contentful reports which could be discussed and contemplated. Nothing mystical about it.

As for Mary, we are told that she kept these things and "pondered them in her heart." Mary had much to think about as she watched events unfold and tied it all in with what the angel had announced to her in the first place. Her place was not going to be an easy one. The reality of Jesus being truly man meant that she had a "truly baby" and would have a "truly little boy" to care for. But his being the Second Person of the Trinity, the One who had always existed from everlasting to everlasting was going to be a puzzle to her day by day. No finite person can ever really understand infiniteness perfectly. Thank God He has carefully let us know that He is also personal, and that we are personal, so that on the side of the person we *can* relate. Mary could relate to the baby and little boy as a Person. As years went on she had much to learn, and to think about, concerning Jesus the Messiah whose coming had been so long waited for.

As a Jewish baby boy, Jesus was circumcised when He was eight days old, and it was at that time his name was given him, the name the angel had announced to Mary nine months before. At the time of Mary's purification, that is, when the baby was forty days old, according to the law of Moses, Joseph and Mary went to the Temple with a pair of turtledoves as a sacrifice. Now these two birds were the poor person's sacrifice ... for those who could not afford a lamb, for the Messiah was brought up in a poor family, experiencing what all the little economies and substitutes meant, in every area of day by day life!

Another thing happened at this time which would have reassured Mary and Joseph again of that which would be hard for them to really feel as *real,* as they cared for this baby. A man in Jerusalem whose name was Simeon, we are told in Luke, had the Holy Spirit reveal to him that he would not die until he saw the Messiah, "the Lord's Christ." Now on the day that Jesus was to be presented at the Temple, Simeon was led by the Holy Spirit to the Temple, and when he saw these two presenting the baby as it was the custom to do, he took the baby in his arms and spoke. Think now, *if this is true*, how marvelous it is in reassuring us, as well as Mary and Joseph! This old man who had seen baby after baby for many years brought to be presented in the Temple, now suddenly takes *this* baby, who does not look special, and looking down at that downy baby head, then up to the Lord, says, "Lord, now lettest thou thy servant depart in peace, according to thy word: For mine eyes have seen thy salvation, which thou hast prepared before the face of all people; A light to lighten the Gentiles, and the glory of thy people Israel."

This is a statement to stun anyone, if they listen to the *content* of what it says, and don't just listen as if it were a few strains of Bach on a violin. He is saying that he can now die. He has been promised that he will not die until he sees the Messiah. Now he says, "All right, God, I can die now. This baby is the One who is coming for the salvation to be complete. He is the One who will be a light to the Gentiles, and a glory to Israel." He is saying—this Jew who spends his time in the Temple and knows the Old Testament Scriptures well—that *this* baby will fulfill the promises to Abraham, and that he knows *the* moment of history has now arrived.

No wonder we are told that Mary and Joseph were full of wonder over what he said. Simeon then blessed Mary and Joseph, and said in prophecy to Mary: "Behold, this child is set for the fall and rising again of many in Israel; and for a sign which shall be spoken against. Yea, a sword shall pierce through thy *own* soul also, that the hearts of many may be revealed."

Yes, there is going to be opposition against Him, and His suffering will affect her too. But it is an echo of what those who have believed have suffered through the ages. Listen to David as he speaks for himself, and prophetically in Psalm 42: "As with a sword in my bones, mine enemies reproach me: while they say daily unto me, Where is thy God? Why art thou cast down, O my soul? and why art thou disquieted within me? Hope thou in God: for I shall *yet praise him* who is the health of my countenance, and my God."

The difference in the suffering of the Messiah is that He suffers at one time in history, for everyone who will believe and accept His substitution for them.

Anna, a prophetess of the tribe of Aser, was very, very old—over 100. She never left the Temple, serving God day and night with fastings and prayers. Anna came along *just* in time to be present so that with Simeon she gave thanks too, and then we are told, "She spake of him to all them that looked for redemption in Jerusalem." You have to picture a spry old woman going around to all the people who she knew really believed God's Word. These were Jews who were looking for the coming of the Messiah, who were looking for the fulfillment of the Old Testament promises in Jerusalem. These were people who took the Scriptures as literally true, not just religiously true, so that they were expecting the prophecies to be fulfilled in *some* period of time—hoping it would be in their lifetime, and in the geographic space of Jerusalem.

You see there were people living then who were like Abraham, Isaac, Joseph, Moses, David, Daniel and his friends, Isaiah, Jonah, Esther, who were faithful to the God of the Bible. As Anna hurried around telling them, they would naturally talk to each other, and encourage each other. People who are a part of "the family" so often know each other and are drawn to a

ELEVEN

special kind of sharing. There would have been a kind of electric current of excitement among them, as well as quiet waiting and prayer. No one was really sure how it would all develop, or what would happen next. After all, a baby takes time to grow up. And when He would be grown, what would He do? If you had stopped one of them to ask, there would not have been a totally clear answer, but some of them were certain enough that this baby was the promised Messiah, that they were sure redemption was near!

TWELVE

John the Baptist, Elizabeth and Zacharias's son, was the one who made a clear announcement for people gathered out in the open air to hear. He was baptizing people who wanted to indicate openly that they were sorry for their sins, and many Jews were gathered together for this baptism. Suddenly he saw Jesus walking toward him and cried out, "Behold the Lamb of God, which taketh away the sin of the world."

A concise statement of historic fact. John is saying to people who know all about the little lambs that have been used as substitutes, who know all about the ark of the covenant in the holy place where the High Priest sprinkled blood on the Day of Atonement: "Behold *the* Lamb of God, which taketh away the sin of the world."

"What lamb?" some child might have asked his mother. "What lamb, Daddy?" another child might have questioned. They saw a man walking toward John. "What does it mean that we are to behold, look at, a *lamb;* this is a man." Many kinds of questions must have swirled through thinking brains, while others might not even have tried to understand. But *some,* a number of people, would have known that John was saying a sentence that had meaning. Some people would have connected this with the promised Lamb of Isaiah's prophecy. Some there that day might have heard Anna thirty years before, come to tell their mothers and fathers that the Messiah had been born. Some might have put together a few things and really "wondered" with their minds, and felt a surge of emotion which would have increased the rate of their heartbeats: "*Could* this be the Messiah?"

John goes on to say something on this order: This is the man about whom I said that there is someone coming who has been *before* me (although Jesus was six months younger). The One who told me to baptize with water, told me that the One upon whom you see the Spirit descending and remaining, the same is He which baptizeth with the Holy Ghost.

In Matthew and Luke we are given the account of how the Holy Spirit descended like a dove to alight upon Jesus, and we are told that at the same time a voice came from heaven, saying, audibly for everyone to hear, "This is my beloved Son, in whom I am well pleased."

John continues, "And I saw, and bare record that this is the Son of God."

At this beginning point in the ministry of Jesus, it is made crystal clear that He *is* the Lamb. Remember that the lamb at the passover time had to be kept for a period of time to be watched to see if it would develop any flaws or blemishes? Jesus is now entering the period of testing, as well as a period of speaking, answering questions, doing miracles, that men might know that indeed God the Son had come to live among them. At the baptism of Jesus, the definiteness of the Triune God was demonstrated as the Son stood there before people, the voice of the Father was heard, and the Holy Spirit came down from heaven in the form of a dove. A "measure of understanding" was unfolded to them at that time, and recorded for us that we too might know.

Matthew tells us that John exclaimed, "I need to be baptized by you, and yet how is it that you come to me?" Jesus explained that He was taking His place with Israel in this act with the believing Jews. He was starting His public life of living without sin for each one for whom His death would be a substitute. In other words He *lived* a perfect life *for* us, as well as dying to take away guilt and punishment as He suffered it for us. As later He was to take men's sins upon Him, so now He is fulfilling a special entrance to the reality of living for men a

TWELVE

life which He could give as a gift. Whatever understanding John had, it was sufficient to cause him to agree to baptize Jesus, and then he observed with his eyes and ears the titanic happening which assured him he had done the right thing, "as the heavens were opened unto him, and he saw the Spirit of God descending like a dove and lighting upon him: and lo, a voice from heaven saying, This is my beloved Son, in whom I am well pleased."

Have you ever heard someone ask, "If God is there, why doesn't he split the heavens and *say* something." He has. He has so many times. He has given us His communication verbally in the Bible. He has spoken to Moses and the prophets, and He spoke 2000 years ago, audibly so that people standing on the banks of that river, which you can visit, heard His voice. He is important enough so that people should listen to what He has *already* said.

Just as Moses was on the mountain for forty days and forty nights, fasting as he came to that important time of receiving the law that men might know what the law of God consisted of, so Jesus was led out into the wilderness to fast for forty days and forty nights in preparation for living a life which would be the *first life* since the law was given to Moses, which would *keep* the law perfectly! And as soon as this time of preparation for the next step of his life was finished, Jesus was hungry, just as Moses had been hungry, after forty days without food.

Now Satan sweeps in with his first big temptation which we know about, "If thou be the Son of God, command that these stones be made bread." That nasty, snide sneer: "If thou be the son of God"! How many times has someone, in your childhood, or when you were an awkward teen-ager, sneered at you: "If ... if ... prove it, prove it, prove it ..." and your face has flushed and you have bitten your lip, and suddenly angry reaction has pushed you into "proving it," whatever "it" was, with words or actions.

Here is the One who created all things! Here is the One who sent the manna. Here is the One who multiplied the bread for Elisha. Here is the One to whom nothing is impossible. "Prove it, prove it." If Jesus had "proved it" He would have

obeyed Satan, and no longer could He have been without
blemish. Thankfully, His answer was, "It is written, Man
shall not live by bread alone, but by every word that
proceedeth out of the mouth of God."

Do you recognize the place from which Jesus was quoting?
An exciting quote from the Old Testament, because it was
one connected with reminding the Israelites about the manna
which God had made miraculously for them, but which
represented the spiritual food, the bread which was coming.
You see Jesus is that bread being pointed forward to. He
could never have been the Bread of Life, if He had made stones
into bread at Satan's command. So He quoted a marvelously
appropriate verse: Deuteronomy 8:2, 3: "And thou shalt
remember all the way which the Lord thy God led thee
these forty years in the wilderness, to humble thee, and to
prove thee, to know what was in thine heart, whether thou
wouldst keep his commandments or no. And he humbled
thee, and suffered thee to hunger, and fed thee with manna,
which thou knewest not, neither did thy fathers know; that he
might make thee know that man doth not live by bread only, but
by every word that proceedeth out of the mouth of the Lord
doth man live."

Then the devil took Jesus up a mountain and showed Him the
kingdoms of this world, stating that he had power to give them
to Jesus if He would only bow down to him, the devil. "Just
worship me, and all these kingdoms will be yours," Satan said.
And Jesus answered with another Old Testament quote. You see
Jesus is emphasizing the fact that the Old Testament *is* the
Word of God, and He is using that which is available as
knowledge to *any* man, knowledge of true truth which God has
had written for men. Jesus is not using the personal knowledge of
which He has an infinite store, but referring to the verbalized,
recorded Word of God. "It is written, Thou shalt worship
the Lord thy God, and him only shalt thou serve." Written
where? Turn to Deuteronomy again—6:13, 14: "Thou shalt fear
the Lord thy God, and serve him, and shalt swear by his name.
Ye shall not go after other gods." For Jesus to bow before
the devil, would be the Son of God bowing before the primary

source of all other gods, the one behind every false god, false religion, false philosophy.

Next the devil took Jesus to a pinnacle of the Temple in Jerusalem. Here is Jesus, the Son of God, standing with Satan, the rebel Lucifer who so long before had tried to gain the victory over God, and who continues to war against Him—directly on the House of God, the Temple into which the ark had been carried so long ago, where the mercy seat was waiting for the final *reality* of the atonement to take place. Standing on this geographic center of the final fulfillment's being recognized, the time only now three years away, Satan says: "Cast yourself down from here. For it is written, He shall give his angels charge over thee, to keep thee. And in their hands they shall bear thee up, lest at any time thou dash thy foot against a stone."

Who is quoting the Bible now? Who knows the Old Testament well enough to twist it with an ugly twist right out of its context to set forth an opposite meaning? Yes, Satan, and Satan's false prophets of the false gods and the false religions often use God's Word twisted out of the context of its meaning to try to prove a directly opposite thing. If Satan tried this with the Son of God, don't you suppose he tries it over and over again with men? It is a clever way to confuse and throw dust—or even acid—in the eyes of men, to blind them to the truth of the very words he is using.

Where does Satan get this quote? Come to Psalms and look up 91:11, 12: "For he shall give his angels charge over thee, to keep thee in all thy ways. They shall bear thee up in their hands, lest thou dash thy foot against a stone."

What is wrong with that? Should Jesus jump?

But if He had, again He would have been obeying Satan. First look at Psalm 91 to see the whole context of this promise of special care by the angels in times of special danger and difficulty. Psalm 91:1-9 are the verses which precede Satan's quote, and these change considerably the challenge of "It is written that angels will take care of you ... jump...."

"He that dwelleth in the secret place of the most High shall abide under the shadow of the Almighty. I will say of the Lord,

He is my Refuge and my fortress; my God; in him will I trust." There is a condition here of staying close to the Almighty God, to trusting *him* alone. "Surely he shall deliver thee from the snare of the fowler, and from the noisome pestilence. He shall cover thee with his feathers, and under his wings shalt thou trust: his *truth* shall be thy sword and buckler." It becomes stronger and stronger, this marvelous psalm, that God will care for His own children, who stay close to Him and to His truth. Jesus, who knew this Psalm very well, knew the context, even as we should know the context when people try to tempt us by misquoting the Bible. Now go on to hear the comforting next verses—comforting to the Son of God as the Word spoke to Him too, as well as to us—"Thou shalt not be afraid for the terror by night; nor for the arrow that flieth by day; nor for the pestilence that walketh in darkness; nor for the destruction that wasteth at noonday. A thousand shall fall at thy side, and ten thousand at thy right hand; but it shall not come nigh thee. Only with thine eyes shalt thou behold and see the reward of the wicked. Because thou hast made the Lord which is my refuge, even the Most High, thy habitation; there shall no evil befall thee, neither shall any plague come nigh thy dwelling."

Thrill, thrill, and thrill again with the sheer wonder of the whole context of that which Satan quoted in part. The Son of God does not need to fear the terror of being tempted by Satan himself right after the weakening effect of forty days and nights of fasting, because the Lord God, the Father, the First Person of the Trinity, is His "habitation"—is his "dwelling place"—is his "refuge." And later, in verse 15, comes this: "He shall call upon me, and I will answer him: I will be with him in trouble; I will deliver him, and honor him." The 91st Psalm speaks to each of us today, as *we* imitate Jesus in getting *our* help from Scripture. Yes, Jesus knows the true context and full meaning of the verses Satan quoted, and knows that staying near to His Father and dwelling with Him in these moments of temptation are the answer. His resisting the temptations was accomplished for us. Don't forget, He was not *living* for us in a special way. However, also, He was showing us how to behave when titanic temptations hit us, when we are offered rationalization for falling, by misquoting the Word of God to ourselves, or having it misquoted by someone else.

What was Jesus' answer to Satan?

"Jesus answering said unto him, It is said, Thou shalt not tempt the Lord thy God" (Luke 4:12). Jesus quoted this from Deuteronomy 6:16: "Ye shall not tempt the Lord your God as ye tempted him in Massah."

The verse in Deuteronomy is referring to the time in Exodus 17, when the Israelites were thirsty and they complained and murmured against Moses, saying, "You just brought us with our children and cattle out of Egypt to kill us with thirst."

And Moses replied to them, "Why do you chide me? Wherefore do ye tempt God?"

Once again it is an amazing place for Jesus to be quoting—marvelous in its reference to the moment when the rock is to be struck by the rod of Moses—a sudden shaft of light. The rock was to be struck *once*, God said, and water would gush out. The people had "tempted God," complaining in impatience, instead of trusting and waiting for Him to take care of all of their needs. Now Jesus says to Satan, "Don't tempt God...." It is not time for Jesus to die. It is not the hour for Him to throw Himself down. He will die *once,* and the "water of life" will gush out, the spiritual water which the water from the rock was looking forward to, even as the manna looked forward to the spiritual bread of life.

It is absolutely indescribable with human words to say what it is like to come upon the tiny details of perfection which God has given us. It is something like studying fine, fine work in gold or silver, or in etching, under a microscope ... tiny perfect details one wonders how anyone could make, and who might see!

In John 3 we have the account of Christ's first discourse. We are told that "there was a man of the Pharisees (religious rulers) named Nicodemus, a ruler of the Jews: The same came to Jesus by night and said unto him, Rabbi, we know that thou art a teacher come from God: for no man can do these miracles that thou doest, except God be with him." Jesus brushed away the compliments and went to the heart of Nicodemus's own need. "Verily, verily I say unto thee, Except a man be born again, he cannot see the kingdom of God."

Jesus is speaking to a religious man who is educated and intellectually knows the Old Testament and all the Jewish ceremonial laws. He is a thinking man, who has come with a question, or many questions, as to who Jesus might be. Jesus answers by telling him that there is a requirement for eternal life, for being in the kingdom of God, and that is as definite and specific as birth. There is a time before one is born, and then a time of birth. This, says Jesus, is what has to happen to a person spiritually. In answer to Nicodemus's further questions, Jesus goes back to a story of Moses and the Israelites in the wilderness which was familiar to Nicodemus, and to other Jews living at that time. There was a time in the wilderness when the Jews were worshiping false gods, that serpents were sent to punish them, and when Moses asked God to help them, Moses was told to take a serpent made of brass, and to hold it up high on a stick, at the same time telling the people that anyone who would look up at the brass serpent would be healed of their snakebites. It was one of those moments of history which is important at the time, but a lesson for later too.

Reminding Nicodemus of this piece of history, Jesus underlines the fact that it really happened, by saying, "As Moses lifted up the serpent in the wilderness," and then goes on to give a future piece of history, a prophecy of His own death which was still about three years away: "*So* must the Son of man be lifted up." After which Jesus Himself, now at the beginning of His ministry, makes very clear the whole purpose of the next three years and the final moment, along with the meaning it could have for Nicodemus, as He went on to say: "That whosoever believeth in him should not perish, but have eternal life." This first discourse commenced Jesus' time of teaching, speaking, doing miracles, and answering questions, with a definite tie-up with the announcement John the Baptist had made when he said, "Behold the Lamb of God which taketh away the sin of the world." Because now Jesus is saying that God the Father so loved the world that He sent His only

begotten son as that Lamb that whoever would believe on Him
would not perish, but would have everlasting life. To make
this crystal clear Jesus goes on to explain that God had not sent
His son to condemn, but to make it possible for people to be
saved, redeemed, born again. He said that "light has come into
the world," and the light would do two things: show up the
sin and evil, but also make it possible for people to see the
solution.

Can't you see? It all ties up with the lamb—Abel's worship
with the lamb, Abraham's understanding of the atonement,
Moses instructing the people in the Passover so that they
understood the substitution of the lamb, that the sons might live,
Isaiah's prophecy. What Jesus is saying to Nicodemus has a
background of history, a base of unfolding teaching through
the years, with no gap, because the Temple with its holy of
holies was right there in Jerusalem.

Immediately after this account we have an account of people
coming to John the Baptist with questions about Jesus. John
says that he himself is not the Christ, but has been sent before
him to prepare the way. He concludes his explanation by stating
that the Father loves the Son and has given all things into the
Son's hand, and that "he that *believeth* on the Son has
everlasting life: and he that believeth not the Son shall not see
life: but the wrath of God abideth on him." John, who said
"Behold," now says "Believe."

So John is dividing the human race into two lines, but not
two different lines than have been given before, simply the
same as Cain and Abel: the unbelieving and the believing. The
same two lines as the worship of the golden calf, and the
worship of the living God. Before he is put in prison and
then beheaded, John makes it clear that the Lamb he
announced as having come, *is* the One who will fulfill the lamb's
work, and provide the redemption necessary for eternal life.

John's time of work has been a short one, but a very fulfilled
one of being the forerunner. He said he was not the Christ, but
that he was to prepare the way. Have you watched a long
race in which the roads are cleared by a car slowly driving
before the commencement of the first racing car—often with

ribbons, perhaps with a loud speaker, closing the road to ordinary drivers, preparing the way for the race? Just so, John the Baptist, son of Zacharias the priest, and Elizabeth, prepared the way that people might be made aware of the One who would follow, so that all eyes would be directed to *Him*. "Behold the Lamb of God which taketh away the sin of the world."

Indeed, behold! and believe.

THIRTEEN

So begins the period of time during which the *Lamb* is being watched by angels and demons, seeking men and scoffers—in many ways the most tense three years in all time.

What does He do for three years? As Lamb He shows forth His perfection, His flawlessness, His sinlessness. As man He shows forth the reality of His having emptied Himself of the glory of heaven to live a day-by-day limited life, being in one place at one time, experiencing hunger, thirst, heat, cold, sorrow, grief, joy. As Shepherd He experiences the search for the lost sheep, the love and yearning over the foolish wandering flock, the willingness to lay down His life for the sheep. As God He experiences that which we never can expect to understand, identifying with those who have been *made* in His image, so that now in their lostness and sin He becomes sin for them, that they might return and be *conformed* to His image. The perfection of love, and the perfection of justice, meeting in a point of history, is more than our finite, limited human minds can ever fathom. Yet, it is in the realm of reality, not of fantasy, and we have been made with minds which *can* think about it and understand sufficiently to *believe* it. We have been given emotions so that we can *feel* the wonder and awe of such a plan.

Both love and justice are words so misused today that it may not be possible to read of the love of God and the justice of God and have any connotation of the words which remotely fits the truth. Language has been robbed by the misuse of words. This has been another clever twisting of the devil's clever lies. Single words can become a lie, without a sentence having been formed at all. God's justice cannot be bribed, and God's love cannot be paid for. God's love is free to all who will come to Him, God's justice is totally fair and the penalty has been met completely.

The plan of God to redeem man is one in which perfect justice is fulfilled, and perfect love expressed.

It took centuries of preparation before the moment came, and now that it is "here," three years seems short. Yet in that three years the Messiah did everything necessary to enable men to "see God." He taught everything that needed to be taught at that time, both in parables and in explanation and answers to questions. He performed miracles which were proof, in every area of proof to tie in with the Old Testament as well as to fulfill the immediate need of help at the existential moment when the miracle was performed. He emphasized that this was true and historical as He constantly referred to the Old Testament as God's authority. These three years were all that were needed to focus history and make it come out of the blur of Satan's lies and men's rebellions.

Listen to Jesus as He specifically points to Himself as the fulfillment of the Messiah in a variety of ways.

"Search the scriptures," commands Jesus, "for in them ye think ye have eternal life: and they are they which testify of me." He goes on with words which cut across the religious scene of then, and now, with a sharp lash: "For had ye believed Moses, ye would have believed me: for he wrote of me. But if ye believe not his writings, how shall ye believe my words?" This is Jesus speaking as he says to religious men then, and now, that the first five books of the Scriptures—the books of Moses—are *true* and are to be believed if men are claiming to believe God. If they are truly believed, then the Messiah will be recognized, because it is in the first five books of the Bible that the Messiah is made clear—the One promised—and also that the base of understanding *anything* is made clear. Oh, Jews and people of the world, says Jesus, if you won't believe what has been given you in Scripture, you won't believe when I speak audibly to you.

Religious leaders then, and now, so fuzzy up or blur the truth that they cause their own ears to be closed to hearing, their eyes to seeing, their minds to understanding. The Pharisees had added so much religiosity contained in additional lists of laws and ceremonies that they couldn't recognize truth when the Son of God spoke audibly to them. This generation is no better. We need to sweep away the hindering dust and smog which has been put between the Old and New Testaments in one form or another. Today the thing of first importance is to believe the writings of Moses—really believe they are true; then, in Jesus' own teaching, we are prepared to believe His words.

Those who say that nothing matters but Jesus, and think of Him as appearing out of nowhere 2000 years ago as a floating mystical happening to be followed, like a ghostly gleam, have not listened to Jesus Himself when He says, "But if ye believe not his writings, *how* shall ye believe my words?"

After the loaves and fish are multiplied by Jesus to feed five thousand people, many flock after Him, but Jesus told them they were coming because they had eaten of the bread. He then says they ought to work not for food that perishes but for that which endures to everlasting life.

Now a sharp and clear question is asked by the crowd, and a specific answer given. "What shall we do to work the works of God?" comes the question.

"This is the work of God, that you believe on Him whom He hath sent." Jesus answers with an unmistakable answer. There is no human work a person can do to be credited with and have earned a place with God. The one *way* is always the same, an inner belief that God has spoken truth in declaring the way to come to Him. They are to believe in the Messiah, having known the five books of Moses and having understood that He is the Lamb, already announced by John.

The crowd next says that their fathers in the wilderness ate manna. What sign, they wanted to know, would Jesus give them? Now they had already eaten of the multiplied bread,

and they had seen other miracles Jesus had performed, but
now Jesus makes it very strong that the miracles of manna and
water in the wilderness were pointing forward to Him.

"And Jesus said unto them, I am the bread of life: he that
cometh to me shall never hunger; and he that believeth on me
shall never thirst."

There was a murmuring against Him ... but always *some*
believed.

What else did He say about Himself? "I am the light of the
world: he that followeth me shall not walk in darkness, but shall
have the light of life."

"Then said Jesus to those Jews which believed on him, If
you continue in my word then are you my disciples indeed;
And you shall know the truth, and the truth shall make you free."

It is because it is *true* that there is a result. There is no
vagueness here but a promise of freedom from lies and false
philosophies or religions which are so binding and which lead
to such dark rooms with no exits!

Again Jesus calls the Pharisees children of the devil: "Ye
are of your father the devil, and the lusts of your father ye
will do. He was a murderer from the beginning and abode not
in the truth, because there is no truth in him. For he is a liar, and
the father of it. And because I tell you the *truth* ye believe me
not."

The issue is clear: either this is truth, or not. A line is drawn
which cannot be straddled. Even though the word "truth" is being
deleted from men's understanding, because of Hegel's whole
relativistic base upon which much of the world operates
today, try to imagine—*if* truth exists, if there is an absolute, if
the world is personal, created by a personal God—*what* the word
truth means. It means by the very nature of the word that there
is something opposite that is not true, and that there can be
no clarity of understanding if there is a muddy mixture.

People try to separate some of the teachings of Jesus as to how
to treat other human beings, and how to live unselfishly, from
His claims to be the Old Testament prophesied Messiah, but
it can't be done.

Jesus says, "I am the door." This is following His telling a

parable of how thieves and robbers try to get into the
sheepfold by another way. Jesus says there is only one door:
"I am the door: by me if any man enter in he shall be saved."

Then He makes it strong with another picture: "I am the good
shepherd: the good shepherd gives His life for the sheep."

And as He is speaking to Jews, those who know their
Scriptures remember Isaiah 40:11: "He shall feed his flock like
a shepherd: he shall gather the lambs with his arm, and carry them
in his bosom, and shall gently lead those that are with young."

Oh, yes, it is *clear.* This is the One who has come to be the
Shepherd of the ones who "like sheep have gone astray," as
Isaiah prophesied. But in case it needs more explanation, Jesus
goes on: "I am the good shepherd.... As the Father knoweth
me, even so I know the Father: and I lay down my life for the
sheep."

And in the same 10th chapter of John: "My sheep hear my
voice, and I know them, and they follow me: and I give unto
them eternal life; and they shall never perish, neither shall
anything pluck them out of my hand. My Father which gave
them me is greater than all; and nothing is able to pluck them out
of my Father's hand. I and my Father are one."

Some picked up stones to stone Him, but many believed.
All were Jews.

His ministry continues with miracle after miracle performed,
question after question answered, teaching after teaching
made plain, and a constantly unfolding explanation that He
had come to die, to suffer, to do that which the Messiah must
do if the *way* is going to become a historical reality of a
substitution being accomplished. In our bird's-eye view,
however, we can only skim past the dusty roads along which
Jesus walks, now with the twelve Apostles, all of whom are
Jewish, and the many disciples following Him. We can listen
briefly to His making known the reality of eternal life, and the
importance of not laying up riches on earth, but laying up
treasures in heaven where they will be permanent. We can
catch His words as He talks about faithful servants, and the good
Samaritan. We can understand the urgency of His teaching a
balance in seeking first the Kingdom of God, rather than

success in earthly things if we believe that He is speaking truth about the past, present, and future. We skim over the miracles of healing, needing to fly *into* the Synagogue in our imaginary flight as some of the healing takes place right there on a Sabbath day. We can marvel as the blind man sees trees for the first time in his life, but far more important, "sees" with spiritual eyes the reality of truth, and who it was who healed him. We can be shaken by the enormity of His drawing the two lines between those who receive Him and those who do not. And by the clarity with which He points to bodily resurrection.

From our vantage point of looking back, however, we are apt not to understand the humanness of the Apostles as they listened and yet did not *really* expect Him to die and rise again. They go up into the borrowed upper room of a house at Passover time, so easily to fall into argument as to who will be "first" in the kingdom, without at all expecting the death of their Messiah as the next historic thing, and their own persecution for years ahead, rather than sharing an immediate totally victorious kingdom. They saw everything Jesus had said to them as covering a very short period of time, rather than centuries.

Come then into the upper room of this ordinary house, where the twelve sit with Jesus at the time all of Jerusalem is celebrating the Passover. The *time* is perfect for the Lamb. It is the celebration of the time when the first lambs died so that the Angel of death would pass over each Israeli house. The Apostles, all Jews, knew very well the lamb had had to die. Now Jesus explains to them as He breaks the bread, that which made it clear this was to be the *last Passover* feast, and the *first Communion*. "Why? What do you mean?" you may well ask.

Think a moment; *if* all this is true, and *if* Jesus has come as the promised Lamb, and *if* He is about to die, is it not the time to have the last Passover which is meant to look back to the night in Egypt when the firstborn sons were saved from death. Why keep looking back to the thing which pictured what the Messiah would do, *after* He has done it? Jesus says as He breaks the bread and blesses it, "Take, eat; this is my body. And He took the cup, and gave thanks and gave it to them saying, Drink ye all of it; for this is my blood of the *new* covenant, which is shed for many for the remission of sins."

You can hardly breathe if you enter into the historic moment of what is taking place. Here is *The Lamb,* making it clear that He is going to die, that those who believe on Him will *live,* not just through a journey in the wilderness, but forever. The breaking and eating of the bread is to remind them that His body is being broken for them. Paul tells us so in 1 Corinthians 12:26: "As often as ye eat this bread and drink this cup, you show forth the Lord's death until He comes."

You see the Lord hasn't taken away the passover feast, He has simply changed it for a taking of bread and wine in remembrance that the *Lamb* did fulfill all the promises of God, and that the communion is to look back to His death and forward to His future coming. Here is the beautiful ending of the Old Covenant and the clear difference of the New!

You see when Jesus comes back, there will be a moment when rather than twelve Apostles taking bread and wine from his hands, every single one of the ones who have believed and been "born again" into the Lord's family, will be receiving communion from His hands.

Jesus tells the men just before He goes out to Gethsemane, "I will not henceforth drink of this fruit of the vine until that day when I drink it new with you in my Father's kingdom." One day we will be together in the whole family of the Lord's people, remembering what the death of *The Lamb* has meant for us. We will have eternal life because of His death. The Son of God became a *Lamb* that the children of men might become sons of God. The exchange is titanic.

In 1 Corinthians 5, there is an admonition to keep the feast, not with the "leaven of malice or wickedness ... but with the unleavened bread of sincerity and truth," and there is this phrase: "For even Christ our passover is sacrificed for us."

Yes, the *time* of Christ's death actually at the passover time is another of the perfect details which makes the continuity with the Old Testament clear and definite.

Now to go into the garden of Gethsemane with Jesus. I have

written in another book* that which I want to repeat here, a paraphrase which I feel is an understanding of Jesus' prayer.

The disciples have been left at a spot behind Him, sprawling on the ground in tiredness, as we know they went to sleep. Peter, who has just declared that he would never deny Jesus, presses on with the two sons of Zebedee, but after awhile Jesus leaves them behind also and goes a bit further alone, asking them to watch with Him.

This is *not* an exaggerated act to focus all eyes on the suffering, but an honest and sincere struggle as Jesus, Son of God and Son of man, faces the final decision of willingness to go to the cross. The separation He faces is not just that of soul from body, but of the Second Person of the Trinity from the other two Persons. The agony of saying "good-bye" at the most heartbreaking moments of life are only a "drop" in an ocean of what would be needed to give us understanding of what Christ faced in the garden. He prayed, "Oh, my Father, if it be possible, let this cup pass from me...." and my paraphrase would be, "Oh, Father, can't you think of another way? Isn't there another way of salvation for people? Can't you redeem them another way? Is this the *only way?*" Jesus—out of all who have ever lived in space and time—was the one Person who had a right to ask this question, because of the price He would have to pay *if there were no other way.* The answer is important to Him not as a line rehearsed, repeated three times to make an emphatic pause in the events as they were recorded. No, it was a real prayer, a real request—and the answer was clearly negative! Jesus received a negative answer to prayer at that agonized moment of pleading. He understands each one of us when we face an answer which is "no," to one of our most frantic pleas. He has suffered beyond anything we could suffer because of His infiniteness and perfection now bowing before the Father willing to become sin for *us,* and to suffer and die, for *us.*

As you, or others whom you know, ask, "Can't there be another way?" "Why aren't there many ways?" It is important to

Everybody Can Know, Francis and Edith Schaeffer, Tyndale House Publishers, Inc., Wheaton, Illinois, 1974.

THIRTEEN

remember that *if* there had been another possible way, the God of love, who loved His own Son from everlasting to everlasting, would have shown that way or ways at that moment, in *time to save His Son from suffering and death.* That there would be other ways paralleling this way, "each as good" as people say, is unthinkable. It again comes down to the question of *truth.* If truth does not exist, then a way of salvation is not needed, for there would be nothing to be saved *from*, or saved *to.* Chance collections of atoms in a chance universe, with no validity to their personalities, no reason for their existence, don't need any help, and there would be no place or person from which help could come.

If it is an impersonal universe, then it is *not* a personal universe. If it is a chance universe, then it is *not* a created universe.

But if the Scriptures are *true,* and we have been created in the image of God—to think and act and feel, to have ideas and choose, to be creative and love and communicate—then our being cut off from communication with God, and cut off from other people, and even divided within ourselves *does* matter. If the Scriptures are true, our being back in a relationship with God, and then back in a relationship with human beings, with a growing reality, is the most important thing of all. And if the Scriptures are *true,* the world was prepared to understand what was needed for a restoration of all we were made for in the first place. The world has been prepared as the years of "unfolding" took place, with a continuity which showed that it *had* to be the death of a lamb, and that there was *no other lamb* sufficient to care for that need, except the Lamb of God.

Jesus prayed three times, each time checking to see whether the disciples were praying with Him, only to find them asleep. What a moment to sleep when there could have been a short time to share the prayer and suffering! But Jesus bore it alone, in the garden, as well as on the cross. He alone took our place. He was separated from the Father for a time that we might be together forever. He walked alone, without friends, in the hands of the soldiers, to be falsely accused.

Then Jesus went to meet the others, and Judas gave Him that kiss of betrayal, the kiss by which he was pointing out to the soldiers which one to arrest. As He goes off now to the long night of torment and ridicule, it is to be as a lamb before her shearers is "dumb." As Pilate says to Him, "Hearest thou not how many things they witness against thee?" Jesus answered him "never a word; insomuch that the governor marveled greatly."

The mocking includes their dressing Him in scarlet robes and a crown of thorns, spitting on Him and taunting Him to tell who had hit Him. They cry out in sarcasm, "Hail, King of the Jews," and yet He kept silent. He who could have answered each taunt by calling on myriads of angels, or by doing many miracles, now keeps silent that *these men,* as well as all others, might have the possibility of redemption, of forgiveness, through His death.

Now He walks out to climb the hill where no substitute will be found as was found for Isaac, because He *is* the substitute, He *is* the Lamb! The time is right—passover; the place is right—where the first atonement at the time of Abraham was demonstrated. Now He sets His face to endure to the very end. And they place Him on the cross, lift it into place between two thieves, and sit down to cast lots for His garments, that the prophecy in Isaiah might be perfectly fulfilled, and anyone knowing that prophecy could recognize what was going on: "They parted my garments among them, and upon my vesture did they cast lots."

As He hangs there, still conscious, he cried out "My God, my God, why hast thou forsaken me?" which David in Psalm 22 had prophesied he would say. He is also forsaken by his friends. They have slipped away in sorrow and confusion. In the moment of the greatest victory of all time and space, the victory over sin and death—the victory over the devil, promised after the fall—in this time during which the victory is taking place, the disciples and friends of Jesus turned away in depression, crushed with disappointment, because of what they thought was defeat.

No one stood there cheering the victory! *No* one brought a calendar and clock to count the days and hours before the resurrection.

The mocking continued as the chief priests and scribes and elders called out, "He saved others; himself he cannot save. If he be the King of Israel, let him now come down from the cross, and we will believe him. He trusted in God, let him deliver him now, if he will have him: for he said, I am the Son of God."

Separated from the Father, Jesus has this temptation thrown in his teeth, the horrible temptation: *"If you can ... prove it."* How thoroughly He could have proven it, and they all could have been flat on their faces in two seconds, but had He come down from the cross, His substitution for us, His fulfillment as the Lamb, would have been destroyed forever, and there would have been no payment for the debts, no "everlasting life" could have been freely given. So He bore the taunting and ridicule for us. Ashamed of Him? Are we ashamed to consider He is who He said He was?

One of the thieves cast the same taunting into His teeth; the other one believed, and Jesus said that that very same day he would be with Him in Paradise. So the two lines of Cain and Abel are drawn vividly by the two crosses on the two sides of Jesus' cross. *His cross divided the world* even as it literally took place right there, that one who believed was on one line, the other on the other!

When Jesus cried with a loud voice and "gave up the ghost," dying by His own will, another tremendous sign was given that this indeed had been the death of the Lamb. The earth-shaking sign of the centuries took place in the split moment of the death of the Lamb—the sign which let it be known on earth and among angels watching in heaven, that His blood was sufficient to forgive sin, to atone for people who would come believing. He Himself was both Lamb and High Priest. For the heavy, heavy curtain, called the "veil of the temple," which separated the holy of holies from the rest of the Temple, was split from top to bottom. This supernatural happening took place in the physical Temple. The veil, or heavy heavy curtain (some say it was eighteen inches thick ... too thick to be cut by anyone trying with knives) was rent into two pieces supernaturally. At the same moment earthquakes shook the ground, the sky was darkened, and some graves opened and believers who had died before came out. The people such as the Roman centurion and others, who stood watching, were afraid, saying, "Truly, this was the Son of God."

You remember what we studied in an earlier chapter, about what was contained in the holy of holies: the ark containing the law, and the mercy seat which was the covering lid, where the blood was to be placed on the Day of Atonement. Now *The Day of Atonement,* which had been looked forward to year after year, has come, and there was never meant to be another lamb's blood brought in. The veil tore in half to open up the holy of holies to anyone who would come "with the blood of the Lamb"—that is to say, anyone believing that Jesus was the Messiah and that He had died as the atonement for him or for her. Jesus Himself was the High Priest, as *well* as the Lamb. *He* entered in by His *own* blood for the people whom He was representing, all who would believe.

In the book of Hebrews we are told that if the blood of animals looking forward to the coming One, sanctified to the purifying of those who came through the centuries in worship, how much *more* shall the blood of Christ, who offered Himself without spot to God, through the eternal Spirit, purge your conscience from *dead works* to serve a living God.

You see it all has been made clear, and the continuity is not broken. In Hebrews a long list of the faithful believers is given, those who desire a "better country," speaking of a heavenly country, and it is shown that they will not be disappointed. The first covenant was made with Abraham, and now Jesus is shown to be "the mediator of the new covenant." And Jesus' blood is referred to as "the blood of sprinkling, that speaketh better things than that of Abel."

Yet, anyone in Jerusalem watching, with history clearly in their memories, could have *thrilled* that day as they saw the darkness, the earthquake, the graves open, the veil ripped from the top to the bottom and Jesus go limp with death all in the *same* moment. They could have recognized that the most important moment in the center of all history was taking place. They could have realized that the work had been accomplished when Jesus said, "It is finished," which would redeem everyone in the past, as well as the living ones, and the yet unborn ones who had believed, were believing, or would one day believe.

Now there is no need of a High Priest as a go-between; all believers can go directly into the presence of God as they pray, communicate, worship, talk to Him day by day wherever they are. And do you know? There has not been a holy of holies, nor offering of sacrificial lambs among the Jews since shortly after that time, to the present. It really has been supernaturally stopped, in spite of men's scoffing and unbelief. Where is the lamb in worship?

FOURTEEN

Is history going anywhere? Endless rises and falls of one
civilization after another. Endless governments rising and
falling, even more rapidly these days than ever before. Is
man, who says he has come from something low into
something now so enthralling high, demonstrating the marvel of a
utopia coming forth out of this height? Are people treating
other people, husbands and wives, parents and children,
neighbors, communities, nations, races, with greater and
greater evidence of progress into unselfish concern and
compassion? Did Dachau take place in some period of time
close to Moses, and has each period of fifty years since then
brought greater beauty in treatment of people by people?
Could history be charted as one straight line rising up on a graph
paper, described by the words at the bottom, "Onward and
Upward Forever," and could the words of "Follow the
Gleam" make practical sense? In the test tube of world events
and personal experiences, can man's evolution into something
ever more wonderful, be proven?

Have you read this morning's paper, or listened to the
news? Have you felt this morning's irritations, fears,
disgruntledness, or even sweeping anger or rebellion?

What *is* the explanation of the past, today, and the future
which "fits"? Is there any key that opens a door of
understanding, or is the universe a round, dark room with no
door to be found, because no door exists? Is there true truth? Or

155

can we only hope for some kind of escape in fantasy, mysticism, or some chemical inducement of flights of floating into an unreal comfort or terror to take us away from the bleak situation?

If God exists and *is* Creator, and if He did make man in His own image, isn't it the *only* possible thing to fit in with logic and reason, as well as love and compassion, that He *explained* to mankind—people—so that they could *understand*? To have a book, Scriptures, the Bible, come from God to man, rather than come from man's groping, is reasonable and *fair,* if God exists. If it is only possible now to set aside preconceived notions, like erasing a blackboard which is full of another teacher's notes so that you can put fresh notes on it, then we can go on and consider the answers of the Word of God as He gives us the truth about where history is going.

God has said that He has given us things which are understandable, so that we are without excuse if we haven't seriously considered true truth.

As Jesus died, and the Temple itself was a scene of proof that His death had been that of the prophesied Lamb, each detail was carried out, as prophets had spoken hundreds of years before. As it was coming close to the Jewish Sabbath day, the soldiers came to break the legs of the ones dying on the crosses, to hasten death, but when they came to Jesus and found He was already dead, not one bone was broken. These men did not know they were fulfilling a prophecy that no bone should be broken when the Messiah died. Again, as they looked on Him after piercing His side with a sword to see if He really were dead, the prophecy in Zechariah was fulfilled which says, "They shall look on him whom they have pierced."

The men who tenderly carried His body away to bury it with the proper linen cloth and spices, were both Jews, Joseph and Nicodemus. Joseph was one of the Pharisees who courageously stepped forward to associate himself with Jesus. His body therefore was laid in a rich man's tomb as Isaiah had said it would be.

The whole historic story of Jonah was a picture of how

156

long Jesus would be in the grave. This length of time was
perfectly carried out. Jesus Himself had answered the Pharisees
once when they asked Him for a sign as to the truth of what He
was saying, with *this* sign which they could so easily have
checked: "For as Jonah was three days and three nights in the
belly of the great fish; so shall the Son of man be three days and
three nights in the heart of the earth." Jesus went on to make
this very strong when He continued, "The men of Nineveh
shall rise in judgment of this generation, and shall condemn it
because *they* repented when Jonah preached to them, but now a
greater One than Jonah is here."

It was not with a desire to see whether this sign were *true*
or not, that some men talked about it, but with a desire to
"squash" what they thought would be an attempt on the part of
the followers of Jesus to deceive the people. Hence at the
request of some leaders, a strong Roman guard was posted
at the tomb, with the opening sealed and the soldiers standing
there with spears. No one could steal the body.

Early on Easter morning, the two women coming to the
tomb were bearing spices for His body. A desperate desire
to do something for the person who is no longer in his or her
body, drives loved ones to bring flowers or do *something* near the
remains of the person's so recently alive body. In those days
the spices gave a satisfying fulfillment of this natural desire.
With no thought of expectation, or feelings of hope, they
dejectedly walked toward the tomb, only to find it—empty! The
stone was rolled away, and the body was not there! It was two
men in "shining garments"—obviously angels, sent as
angels had been sent to announce His coming to Mary
thirty-three years before, who now told the women that the One
for whom they were looking among the dead, was not dead but
alive. "He is not here, but is risen: remember how he spake
unto you when he was yet in Galilee, saying the Son of man
must be delivered into the hands of sinful men, and be crucified,
and the *third* day rise again."

Then they remembered. Then the flood of remembrance
flowed over them, bringing the kind of ecstatic relief and joy
that no one can know who has not experienced having a son or a

husband who has been reported dead, appear on the doorstep, back from the war! Except that this was *more* than that, for they had *seen* Him die, and had given up all hope of His having been the real Messiah because the sight had so shattered them. All certainty of the truth of what He had said must now have flooded over them, drowning out the sorrow and depression. Everything would not fall into place in their understanding immediately; it would take time, but this they were now sure of—He really was the Son of God; He was, after all, the Messiah. He *had* done just what He had told them He was going to do—He had died. It was now three days, and He had risen. He was alive.

Imagine the excitement and awe, the trembling of knees and beating of hearts as these two went to find other disciples to tell. Was there a shout? Was there a scream of joy? No, the news was too stunningly "impossible," and the first reaction was one of unbelief. "And their words seemed to them as idle tales, and they believed them not."

Peter ran impulsively as fast as he could go to see for himself. John, the younger man, outran him. Peter beheld the linen clothes, laid by themselves—the graveclothes folded up and left behind, no longer needed! Peter turned to go away, "wondering in himself at that which had come to pass." Yes, wondering, marveling, thinking about it, turning over in his mind all that he remembered that Jesus had said, but which he had so quickly forgotten at the time of Jesus' trial and death. "After all, it was *true* ... really true ... it has been literal not figurative ... Jesus really did die and then rise again ... I never thought it was going to be so literal ... how could it be ... it is all too much to take in ... we must think about it.... I wonder what comes next ... I must talk to the others ... I wonder if we'll see Him ... where is He now?" What do you suppose would be going through Peter's mind— Peter, the impulsive, lovable Jewish fisherman who had had such ups and downs of feeling. Peter, who had declared he would never deny Jesus, and who had so quickly become ashamed or fearful and had denied Him three times before the cock crowed—what a tumbling rush of thoughts must have gone through his mind as his feet took him to his next place. On the other hand, we are told that John understood and believed.

On the road to Emmaus, two of the disciples were walking from Jerusalem and talking dejectedly to each other about their disappointment. They had been so sure that Jesus had been the Messiah—but now their hopes were dead, and the expectation that history had really been going somewhere, that the prophecies had really been fulfilled, was now gone. What was there to live for, what could they ever believe again? At this time Jesus, the risen Messiah, walked up beside them, "But their eyes were holden that they should not recognize Him" (God blinded them as far as recognition went for that time).

Jesus asked, "Why are you so sad? What are you discussing, as you walk, which makes you so very sad?"

And Cleopas answered, "Are you a stranger in Jerusalem? Haven't you heard the things which have taken place these days?"

"What things?" asked Jesus.

And they replied, "Concerning Jesus of Nazareth, which was a prophet mighty in deed and word before God and all the people: and how the chief priests and our rulers delivered him to be condemned to death, and have crucified him. But we trusted that it had been *he* which should have *redeemed* Israel; and beside all this, today is the third day since these things were done." Then they went on and told him that some of the women had visited the tomb and had found him gone, and said they had a vision of angels who told them he was alive.

Jesus replied to them, "Oh, fools and slow of heart to believe all that the prophets have spoken. Ought not Christ to have suffered these things, and to enter into glory? And beginning at *Moses* and the prophets, Jesus expounded to them *all the scriptures* concerning himself."

What a fantastic explanation that must have been. Jesus Himself going over the Old Testament to point out all the things which spoke of His birth and life, death and resurrection. He showed them the continuity—He explained to them the fulfillment of all that had been promised for the redemption of the people of God. Jesus showed that the "new testament," the "new covenant," was a continuous line from the "old testament," the "first covenant," and showed them how it all fitted together. He did it from the Scriptures, so He did not give them anything we cannot find in Scripture. Jesus was showing that there was not a "new religion" about to be started, but that everything that had happened had already been told by the prophets, and was a fulfillment. *Jesus* was explaining that Christianity is Jewish. Jesus was showing how all the details fit together perfectly. Jesus was discussing history and prophecy as *truth* about Himself, as well as underlining the fact that the Old Testament is all important as the Word of God from which to find out facts and obtain understanding.

It was not until they stopped and ate together, when Jesus broke bread and blessed it and gave it to them, that "... their eyes were opened and they knew him." Then He vanished out of their sight.

You see Jesus is now in His resurrected body. He is not a "ghost," but has His changed body, which we will see He allows many to see, so they will be able to *know* it is real. In 1 Corinthians the definiteness of His body as a "hope" to all who are believers, both Old and New Testament believers and all who will follow through the centuries, is given thus: "If in this life only we have hope in Christ, we are of all men most miserable. But now is Christ risen from the dead, and become the firstfruits of them that slept. For since by man came death, by man came also the resurrection of the dead. For as in Adam all die, even so in Christ shall all be made alive."

Jesus walked among men for forty days after His resurrection, making known the reality of His risen body, that people would *know* what He meant by "firstfruits." If an apple is seen to develop on a tree, it is generally assumed that this is an apple tree, and the fruit coming the next year will be more apples. Jesus says that *His* risen body is the first one. He is the first One to have a resurrected body, and this body is an example of what everyone's will be like when they come forth from the grave, at the day when Jesus comes back again. Some will be alive at His coming, and the believing ones will be changed at

FOURTEEN

that time, in a moment, in a twinkling of an eye, passing straight into the changed everlasting bodies without dying.

These forty days are important ones for a number of reasons, but one reason is the specific unfolding to people from that time on, as to what the everlasting body will be like. By the things He did Jesus made this known, by letting people find out and tell each other. Finally the writers chosen to give the account with infallible inspiration in the New Testament, *recorded* what we need to know for our hope, expectation, and excitement as we wait for the future to arrive!

What sort of things did He make known? His body could appear in a room without the need of opening doors and coming through. He suddenly appeared in the midst of His disciples when the doors were shut, and said, "Peace be unto you." After speaking, He showed them His hands and His side to show them that the wounds were still there, and that it was the *same* body which had died three days before on the cross. His disciples were filled with gladness when they saw Him—not with fear or doubt. However, Thomas was not there at the time when Jesus came, and when the other disciples told him they had seen the Lord, he declared, "Except I myself shall see in his hands the print of the nails, and thrust my hand into his side I will not believe."

It was eight days later when the disciples were again in the room with the doors shut, when Jesus stood suddenly in their midst again and said, "Peace be unto you." This time Thomas was there. Then Jesus told Thomas to put forth his finger and touch Him, saying, "See my hands." Again He said, "Reach out your hand and thrust it into my side." Jesus did not say, "Just *look* at me," He said, *"Touch* me to see that I am not a spirit or a ghost. A spirit does not have flesh and bone." He is declaring that He is *not* like Moses was on the mount of transfiguration, who was a spirit. Nor is He even as Elijah was, because Elijah did not have a resurrected body. He was demonstrating exactly what our resurrected bodies will be like, as they are to be of flesh and bone. We can touch each other, not just speak and look, but touch, shake hands, be together in our bodies, forever.

Jesus remarks to Thomas that the ones who will believe these things without seeing with their eyes as Thomas has done, will be particularly blessed. He is talking about each of *us* who have believed the accounts, but have not yet seen with our eyes, nor felt with our hands. Right after telling this story, John goes on to say that Jesus gave many other proofs which were seen by the disciples—things which are not written down. But that that has been written has been recorded "that ye might believe that Jesus is the Christ, the Son of God, and that believing ye might have life through his name."

The true truth has not been hidden from the eyes and ears of men, but made known so that they *could* have an opportunity to understand and believe, and have the result of being assured that death is *not* the end, and that the body will *not* be destroyed forever, but that we can look forward to *life* forever and ever in bodies like Christ's resurrected body.

Jesus showed Himself again to the disciples at the sea of Tiberias. The men who were there were Thomas called Didymus, and Nathanael of Cana in Galilee, and the sons of Zebedee, and two others, along with Simon Peter. Peter had said that he was going out fishing, and the others said they would go with him. They went immediately into a ship, but although they fished all night, they caught nothing. You can imagine them tired and disappointed as the first streaks of light changed the dark of the sky, and then the sun began to bring more color. Suddenly their eyes caught sight of a man on the shore who was calling out to them, "Children (or sirs), have you caught any fish?" And they shouted back an answering, "No."

Then they heard the man telling them, "Cast your net on the right side of the ship, and you will find something." They did what He had said, and cast their net on the other side, and there were so many fish in the net they were not able to draw it in.

John 21:7 says: "Therefore that disciple whom Jesus loved said unto Peter, It is the Lord." Now when Simon Peter heard that, he quickly wrapped his fisherman's coat around him, because he had been fishing naked, and jumped into the sea. The other disciples came on in a little ship, for they weren't far out from the land, dragging the net with the fish in it.

FOURTEEN

As soon as they all got to land, they saw a lovely sight. In the early morning light a breakfast welcomed them, for Jesus had made a little fire and the coals were glowing just right for cooking. Already He had laid fish and bread on the coals. So Jesus in His resurrected body had cooked the breakfast over a campfire He had Himself made. Before they ate together, Jesus talked to them, using the fish as an illustration. "Bring here the fish you caught," He said. Simon Peter went up and drew the net to land, full of great fishes, 153 of them in all, and yet the net had not broken.

Then Jesus said, "Come and eat," and the disciples didn't dare ask, "Who are you?" because they knew very well it was Jesus, but they really must have been amazed to have him prepare this meal, then sit and break bread and eat with them, serving them bread and fish. So you see Jesus is making it clear that the resurrected body can eat. Another time He ate fish and honeycomb to let them know He was not just a spirit, after which He said that all the things which were written in the law of Moses, and in the prophets and in the psalms concerning himself, had to be fulfilled. At this time He taught them clearly from the Scriptures again, and they could see it in perspective now as He spoke to them in His resurrected body. He told them that it had been written that Christ was to suffer and rise from the dead the third day, and that now repentance and remission of sins should be preached in His name among all nations, *beginning* at Jerusalem.

The miracle of the many fish in the net was Christ's last miracle, and it seems to tie in with His having said that other time to them, "I will make you fishers of men." The two things go together. He will enable them to "catch men" in the heavenly net, so to speak, that men might have everlasting life. And He tells them they are to start by preaching the truth of how to solve the problem of being cleansed from sin, and that this truth is to be preached first in Jerusalem, but also to all nations.

He then tells them that they are to wait in Jerusalem until God the Father sends special power from on high to them. He led them out as far as Bethany, and then lifted up His hands and blessed them.

Now while He was blessing this little group of Jewish men, who had believed Jesus was the Messiah, and had come now to understand what His death meant to them, and to all who would come to Him, suddenly He began to move up, up, up—into the heavens above, and on into heaven. As He disappeared into the clouds, you can imagine that their heads would still be thrown back watching in astonishment.

However, they had had several strong things to prepare them for this moment. His teaching for three years was, after all, in their minds, even though His death had knocked them into complete forgetfulness because of shock and sorrow and a lack of understanding. Now they had the three years of teaching to remember, *plus* the marvel of having had the resurrection proven to them by what the book of Acts calls, "many infallible proofs." He was seen at one time by 500 people, and He was seen over and over again by the same people, in different circumstances. He had told them that the Holy Ghost would come upon them to help them, to comfort them, and to give them power for the work He had told them to do.

So as they stood gazing up and watching Him disappear, it was with very different feelings than they had had when they watched Him die. The men and women were ready now to tell others that which they were convinced was *true,* and no amount of persecution was going to stop them. There was a tremendous difference between their behavior right after Christ's death, and now. Why? Because they had become convinced by the resurrection that it was all *true.* They were not risking their lives on the basis of mystical feeling or because of a "new religion," but because they were sure now that the Old Testament and the life, death, resurrection and teaching of Jesus all fit together.

Who felt this way? Well, the Jews who had believed. Jews from every walk of life—fishermen, doctor, lawyer, religious leaders, taxgatherers, housewives, sellers of purple, tentmakers, dress makers—some from every age group and social and educational group. A minority, but a cross section, of Jews were convinced that Abraham, Moses, David, Daniel, had looked forward to the Messiah, and that now they were living in the period of history when He had come, and died, and that they had to let this fact be known.

Difficult times were ahead for these believing Jews. Nero would soon be ruling and persecution was going to come from all sides, but two things were given them which were going to enable them, and any other believers through the centuries ahead, to have strength and courage to keep on.

One was that which the angels said to the disciples as they continued to look up, with their eyes glued to the place where they had last seen Jesus, hoping He might come back into sight. Two men in white apparel stood by them and said, "Ye men of Galilee, why stand ye gazing up into heaven? This same Jesus, which is taken up from you into heaven, shall so come in *like manner* as ye have seen him go into heaven."

It was a titanic promise that Jesus would come back, some day, as definitely as He had gone. This same body would be seen again by them, but meantime they needed to do what He had told them to do. They had an important task. But they had the great help of this promise as a comfort and an expectation.

The other help that they had was the possibility of praying and waiting together for the coming of the Holy Spirit. From this time on, the Holy Spirit would indwell each believer. Later in the New Testament it is made clear that now the believing people are to be "the temple of the Holy Spirit." Communication with God the Father has been opened up by the death of the *Lamb,* and the Holy Spirit can now also dwell in people cleansed by His blood. No longer do people have to come looking forward to redemption at a future point of history, but the blood of the Lamb *is,* in the present, effective in opening up close contact and communication with God.

The disciples went back to Jerusalem, and when they arrived they gathered in an upper room—the Apostles, the women, Mary the mother of Jesus, and also his brothers. "These all continued with one accord in prayer and supplication."

What were they praying for? They were praying that the Comforter, the Holy Spirit whom Jesus had promised, would come to be with them, and they were praying for a replacement for Judas, who had betrayed Jesus and had committed suicide after that. Two men were suggested, and they prayed and cast lots, asking God to cause the lot to fall upon the person of His choice. With the new Apostle, Matthias, all twelve were still Jews.

"And they prayed and said, Thou, Lord, which knowest the hearts of all men, show whether of these two thou hast chosen" (Acts 2:24).

They were showing very vividly the difference between their time of bewilderment after Christ's death, and their understanding now that He had risen and ascended. They were commencing a time when each believer was a priest, and each one could come directly to the Father in prayer in the name of Jesus, the Messiah.

Now the Redeemer had come. He had died to redeem His people from all their iniquities, and now the believers were commencing the centuries of waiting for His second coming. But they were not waiting selfishly. At this moment they were waiting for the Holy Spirit to give them power and courage to *live* in the light of the truth of what had happened, and of what is still coming, and while living this way, to help them make this truth *known* with verbalized explanations to others.

FIFTEEN

When the Holy Spirit did come on the day of Pentecost, he came to these men and women who such a short time ago had been so very alone and sad and without hope, but now were waiting so full of trust in the promise of Jesus, and expectant of its being fulfilled. "I will send you the Comforter, when I go," Jesus had said. Now they are looking forward to His arrival.

There was audible sound of the arrival of the Holy Spirit that first time He came to dwell in believers. The sound came suddenly, from heaven, as the sound of a rushing wind, and it filled the house where they were sitting. Then a little tongue of flame appeared above each head, and at this time He entered them and they began to speak. Many people of other language groups were there in Jerusalem, and as they flocked to hear these people, each one heard what was being said, in his own tongue. It was not a babble of un-understandable sounds, but the accurate language of each person. Was the miracle in the ears of the listeners? It was like instantaneous translation for those who heard, because they could understand the words. It was a demonstration, so it seems to me, that some from *every* nation, kindred, tongue and people *will* hear with understanding the true truth. The beginning of the "telling others" which was going to take place in the centuries to follow, was a vivid miniature picture of what was coming.

The Holy Spirit would come, as a breeze, a wind, moving the people in whom He would dwell, and moving others as their lives would be affected. He would not be seen with physical eyes, but the effect upon lives would be seen. Even as poplar trees are in movement with the slightest breeze, so lives "blown by the Spirit" would be alive, not dead, in a noticeable way. Jesus had said to Nicodemus in His first talk with him, "The wind bloweth where it listeth, and thou hearest the sound thereof, but canst not tell whence it cometh, and whither it goeth: so is everyone that is born of the Spirit."

Surely Nicodemus was among the other believers when the mighty rushing wind was heard, and the Spirit came for this special beginning of the period of time between Christ's death and His second coming. Don't you suppose Nicodemus *remembered* those words of Jesus to him, and suddenly understood in a very real way? Yes, the work of the Holy Spirit in helping unbelievers to understand, and in helping believers to do what God would have them do, and to grow in understanding, is always to be compared to wind—no one can "see" with their physical eyes the Spirit Himself, but His effects are as definite as the effects of breezes, light winds, or strong winds.

Then as the flames appeared above each person, it was a picture of the spiritual reality which would follow. Men and women were to speak with tongues of fire in giving powerful, Spirit-filled messages when explaining true truth to others. They were going to be able to do this because the Holy Spirit would now be dwelling in each one of them. Remember Solomon's dedication of the Temple? Remember that after that, the Lord appeared unto him and said, 1 Kings 9:3: "I have heard thy prayer and thy supplication, that thou hast made before me: I have hallowed this house, which thou hast built, to put my name there for ever; and mine eyes and mine heart shall be there perpetually." God promised to dwell in the Temple, and to be found of His people there—but only the High Priest could go into that holy of holies where the presence of God was, and only on the basis of bringing the blood of the lamb for the people waiting outside.

Now, the Holy Spirit has come to live in *each* believer, and at this time they were Jews, children of Abraham, who

168

understood the history and would marvel at what they would soon come to understand, as Paul later spoke to the Corinthians in 3:16: "Know ye not that ye are the temple of God, and that the Spirit of God dwelleth in you?" And again in 6:19: "What? know ye not that your body is the temple of the Holy Ghost, which is in you, which ye have of God, and ye are not your own? For ye are bought with a price, therefore glorify God in your body and in your spirit, which are God's."

For those who had felt what it felt like to be outside the Temple waiting for the yearly time of atonement to be over, knowing that they could *not* approach the holy place, it was earth-shaking to realize that now that *The Lamb* had died in history, and the event was in the past, accomplished, from now on each believer could not only approach God the Father in communication, conversation, prayer, at any time, without a go-between, but that now the Holy Spirit, the Third Person of the Trinity, would dwell in them. "Ye are bought with a price" refers to the terrible price the agony of separation from the Trinity, and dying on the cross, had cost the Messiah. The price has been paid that those who believe might be *completely* forgiven and cleansed from their sin. The reality of the completeness of the washing away of sin through the blood of the Lamb, the Messiah, is proven in this very place—each one who believes and accepts what the Messiah has paid for them, is washed thoroughly enough so that the Holy Spirit can live there. Each one who believes is as special to God as the holy of holies!

Huh! You may think, surely there are a lot of *dirty* clean people! "I know a lot of people who say they believe all this, and they don't seem so all-fired good," you may say.

Does all this mean that people become suddenly perfect when they come on the basis of the Lamb who died to open the way for men to come to God? Does this mean that the "lost lambs" are perfect as soon as the Shepherd brings them into His fold?

To clarify this it is important to recognize that the Bible teaches that there are three aspects of salvation from sin and the results of sin. First when a person understands what God has made clear, and accepts the solution that God paid so dearly to make available, and accepts what has been accomplished on the cross two thousand years ago, that person immediately is forgiven and cleansed from the guilt of all his or her sin. The guilt is gone right away, forever.

The third thing that takes place when a person is "born again" as Jesus told Nicodemus he must be, is that if his plane crashes, or a truck hits his car, or cancer suddenly strikes her down, or the bombs fall, and the soul is separated from the body, the teaching, "absent from the body is to be present with the Lord," applies immediately. The true new birth needs nothing added to assure the person of eternal life. The thief on the cross had no time to live a special life after he believed on Jesus, yet Jesus said, "This day you will be with me in Paradise." And when Christ comes back, one's body is immediately raised from the dead.

Yes, I did say "third" on purpose. The second thing that takes place is a gradual thing. The second thing that happens is that a person is saved from the power of sin in his or her life, and that is called "sanctification," which is a gradual process. There is growth, there is change, but *no* person becomes perfect in this life. When Jesus comes back, we will be perfect, but until He does, there are no perfect people. Therefore when the Holy Spirit dwells within people, they do not become *perfect.* He can dwell there because they have been so perfectly washed clean of guilt, and are ready to go to be with the Lord in the split second of death. But the day-by-day life is a battle. Satan is an enemy who has not yet been "bound"—he is like a lion roaring around the world "seeking whom he may devour." Satan's whole thrust is one of destruction, and what he tries to destroy in the "born-again one" is peace, joy, longsuffering, gentleness, meekness, kindness, and so forth.

You see when the Holy Spirit lives in people, they are meant to allow Him to bring forth "fruit" through them. "The fruit of the Spirit is: love, joy, peace, longsuffering, gentleness, goodness, faith, meekness, temperance." Paul explains this to the Galatians, and goes on to say, "If we live in the Spirit let us also walk in the Spirit."

FIFTEEN

Perfect? *No.* But there is help to bring growth, and there is help in battling Satan as he tries to attack in order to cause worm-eaten, blighted, wizened things to appear in the place of fruit.

So the Holy Spirit came, and the believers began to speak with boldness to others concerning the truth. Peter, who had slunk away and had been afraid even to admit to a serving girl that he was a follower of Jesus, now was the one to stand up before thousands of people and *preach.*

Peter preached with explanation of what had happened, going back to the Old Testament and making it clear. And as a result, that day 3000 Jews believed. Three thousand is a large number to believe in one day at *any* period of history, but this was when it would be *most* unpopular and dangerous, yet 3000 believed and were willing to make it known among friends and family by being baptized and counted as among the believers.

The apostles preached and had been given special power in the Holy Spirit to heal people so that in this most difficult moment of history, when such a tiny number had been given the work of making truth known in Jerusalem, Judea, and "the uttermost parts of the earth," they might be helped to realize that what was being said was *true.* Remember that the New Testament had yet to be written, so people had nothing to take with them back into their homes and study. The only written scripture was the Old Testament, during the first days after the resurrection.

As Peter and Stephen and others preached they always referred to "The God of Abraham, Isaac, and of Jacob, the God of our fathers...." and they *explained* so that people would know the continuity of history, of the promises and the fulfillments. Don't forget that it was not a very impressive group of men—just twelve Apostles, and they were men known to everyone—not superbeings from another planet. Here were fishermen, a taxgatherer. What could *they* know?

However the number of believers was rapidly growing as the Holy Spirit opened people's eyes of understanding, as honest, sincere seekers came to hear the truth, and as the men preached, not in their own power, but in the power of the Holy Spirit.

Persecution came violently and immediately. Stephen was stoned to death, even while he was preaching, and a man standing back in the crowd, holding the coats of the men stoning him, was Saul—who later was to be so completely changed and convinced, that even his name was changed, to Paul. Peter was thrown into prison and as the whole group of believers prayed for him to be released, an angel came in the night and unfastened his chains and led him out. The cool air of the outdoors caused Peter to know it was not a dream, but when he came to knock at the gate of the very house where they were praying, the people could not believe the little girl who ran to tell them Peter was there; they found it hard to believe the answer to their prayer had *really* taken place.

Saul who had so harshly persecuted the believing Jews, who himself was "breathing out threatenings and slaughter against the disciples of the Lord," was on his way to Damascus to search for more men and women to bring bound as prisoners, into Jerusalem. It was on this journey, by foot, to increase the persecution, that suddenly a great light shone around him, and he fell to the earth, and heard a voice saying, "Saul, Saul, why persecutest thou me?" And Saul said, "Who art thou, Lord?" and the Lord said, "I am Jesus whom thou persecutest."

And then Saul, trembling and astonished, said, "Lord, what wilt thou have me to do?"

When he got up to his feet, he found he had been blinded, and for three days and nights Paul did not eat or drink, nor see, but men led him to a house in Damascus. Now the Lord spoke to a man named Ananias in a vision and told him to go to a street called Straight and talk to this man Saul. Ananias knew all too well the history of Saul's persecution of believers, so he explained that this man had authority to take prisoners among the believers, and of course he didn't want to go—he was afraid. However the Lord made it known to Ananias that he was to be the one to talk to Saul and give him his sight back *and* baptize him. The Lord had said that Saul was a "chosen vessel" unto Him, who would preach to Gentiles and kings, as well as to the children of Israel.

This same Saul, who became Paul, later speaks to the Corinthians so strongly about himself, as he warns them of false teachers who are deceitful and not true to the continuity of true truth. He says in 2 Corinthians 11: "Are they Hebrews? so am I. Are they Israelites? so am I. Are they the seed of Abraham? so am I." So he establishes himself as a Jew with a strong Jewish family background. Then he goes on to give an account of the persecutions and the hardships he himself has borne: "in labors more abundant, in stripes above measure, in prisons more frequent, in deaths oft. Of the Jews five times received I forty stripes save one. Thrice was I beaten with rods, once was I stoned, thrice I suffered shipwreck, a night and a day I have been in the deep (more than twenty-four hours in the deep water!). In journeyings often, in perils of waters, in perils of robbers, in perils by my own countrymen, in perils by the heathen, in perils in the city, in perils in the wilderness, in perils in the sea, in perils among false brethren; in weariness and painfulness, in watchings often, in hunger and thirst, in fastings often, in cold and nakedness."

He was *not* turned aside by all the suffering, persecution, and difficulty, but rather goes on to tell of the marvel of all he has come to understand, about the Lord and all that is ahead, marvels which were so exciting that he goes on to tell of a fresh difficulty he had which "kept his feet on the earth" so to speak, which kept him from being too excited to go on with his work.

You see he says he was given a "thorn in the flesh"— something that Satan sent to try to buffet him, and which the Lord did not take away, "lest I be exalted above measure." Paul prayed three times that this "thorn" might be removed, but he was *not* healed. Why? Was his faith not strong enough? No, that cannot be the answer. It was that the victory of answered prayer, the victory against Satan in this particular attack in Satan's battle in the heavenlies, was to be *this:* "And he (the Lord) said unto me, My grace is sufficient for thee: for my strength is made perfect in weakness."

Paul has been absent from his body, and present with the Lord, for many centuries now. The day is coming, when Jesus comes back, that Paul's body will be raised from the dead, and *we* will be able to see him and shake hands with him. Eternity is going on forever and ever and ever in perfect bodies with no suffering, so sadness, no sin, no difficulties. In the perspective of present time as contrasted with eternity, *what* was more important? Some of the answers to prayer Paul had in which circumstances were suddenly changed, or the answer he had of being given "strength made perfect in weakness"? Multiply that by the thousands upon thousands who have been helped to have this same victory in the midst of prison or physical illness, and have found it to help them understand the battle involved, and the importance of the variety of victories. Satan will one day be cast down entirely, but until then he continues to do what he did to Job. There are two kinds of victory the Messiah came to give in this life—and Paul knew them both. Paul surely did not have a smooth, easy life with all suffering removed. The criterion of judging whether a person is a child of God by the health, wealth, and ease of their life and "lot" on *this* earth, is a false one. The battle and the victories are more complicated than that—but the final victory *is* coming. History is going somewhere, and as our "bird flight through the Bible" rushes on, we will catch a glimpse of what is ahead.

Before peeping down at a special happening in Peter's life which was to clarify *his* understanding, we need to pause for an explanation which will prepare *us* to realize what is taking place. Peter needed to be startled out of his prejudices and misconceptions, as he and the others could not imagine their God being interested in Gentiles. Surely he must have remembered Jonah's commission to go to Nineveh, as he knew the Old Testament Scriptures, but he could not fathom the depth of reality of God's love and compassion for all mankind, in spite of Jehovah's having reiterated His love over and over again in the Scriptures.

It was Peter who was asked to go and explain the truth to a Gentile—and it was an order that shocked him.

FIFTEEN

The situation began with the man Cornelius who lived in Caesarea, a centurion of the group of soldiers called the Italian band. This Roman soldier was known as a good man who gave alms to the poor, and prayed to God continually. One day at about the ninth hour, he had a vision, and in this vision an angel of God came to him and told him that his prayers had been heard by God, and that God was aware of his earnestness in giving alms, and that there was a man who would soon come to him to tell him what he should do. Here was a man, seeking God with all his heart, and the promise that he will surely find Him is being carried out. We are permitted in this case to have the "curtain drawn back" as we are told of his vision, and we are told of how God answered his prayers. The angel said that a man named Peter was living by the seaside with a tanner named Simon, and that he would be coming to tell him what to do. You see he was going to be told the true history of what had happened, and of what he must do to be a child of God.

Meantime we are taken to Peter's room. This is like a Chinese theater—we are given glimpses of two "inside scenes" at once, miles apart. It is not fanciful, however; it is history. We are being given history which is important for our own understanding, history only God could give in inspired Scripture.

Peter was praying in the city of Joppa when he also had a vision. In his vision a thing that looked like a big sheet, tied by four corners, seemed to descend from heaven and it came right beside him. Inside this sheet when he looked at it, he saw all sorts of animals, wild beasts, creeping things, and birds. Then he heard a voice saying, "Arise, Peter, slay and eat."

Now Peter was shocked and replied, "Not so, Lord, for nothing common or unclean hath at any time entered my mouth." In other words Peter was saying, "I don't eat anything that is not kosher. I always eat kosher food. I am a good Jew, and I'm not going to now start eating nonkosher."

Then the voice spoke to him a second time and said, "What God has cleansed, that call not thou common."

This took place *three* times. God made sure that Peter understood that He was speaking to *him.* Peter was not allowed to think it was just a mistake. The repetition was for strong emphasis which would give Peter certainty. Why? Because Peter was going to be asked to do something which was unthinkable to a good Jew. He was going to be asked to do something which was against all his background. He would have been sure to say, "No" to a request which was coming in a few minutes, had not God prepared him so specifically. Peter was going to be asked to go and talk to a Gentile, a goy, an uncircumcised person about the things of God. This was a titanic request to a good Jew of that time.

Whatever division had been brought about by people believing that Jesus was the Messiah, up to this time was only a division between Jew and Jew. Gentiles had had nothing to do with it at all. Everything that had happened up to this point in Jerusalem and Judea and the surrounding places, had happened among Jews. All those 3000 who had believed that day that Peter had preached, all those who listened and discussed in the Synagogues and around the Temple, had been Jews. It was a Jewish discussion—a Jewish difference of opinion.

Now while Peter sat there in Simon's seaside house in Joppa, stunned by what he had seen and heard in the vision, suddenly he is told that some men are asking for him at the gate. There are three men looking for him. As Peter thought again about the vision, the Spirit spoke to him and said clearly that three men were looking for him and that he was to *go with them,* because He (the Spirit) had sent them.

Now Peter, well prepared, goes to meet the men, and to hear their story of Cornelius's vision, and of their commission to go and get a man named Peter to tell them what he should do. They said God had told Cornelius through an angel to get Peter. So Peter acquiesced, and brought them in to stay overnight, so that he could leave with them early the next morning to go to Caesarea.

The next morning they went back to Caesarea and when Cornelius went out to meet Peter he fell down to his knees and worshiped him, but Peter said, "Get up, I'm just a man like you are"—and so they went inside the home together. Cornelius had been so excited that God was sending him someone to tell him the details of truth and what he needed to do, that he had gathered all his family, relatives, and friends together, so there was quite a crowd there waiting with a tremor of excitement, an air of expectancy. Here was a man God had sent with a special message. They were prepared to believe God's word, because they evidently had already believed God's word to Cornelius.

Peter started his explanation to them by saying, "Now you know it is unlawful for a Jew to keep company, or to come unto one of another nation; but God has showed me that I should not call any man common or unclean." After that he asked what they had sent for him for, and so Cornelius repeated the story of his vision in which an angel had told him to send for Peter and had said that Peter would tell him what he needed to know. So now, says Cornelius, we are waiting to hear all the things that God has told you to tell us.

After that Peter opened his mouth and began to speak to them about Jesus. He told them that which was talked-about knowledge at that time, and put it into history, as he told of how Jesus brought the word of God to the children of Israel, and that He, Jesus, was the One of whom all the prophets had spoken (the prophets who had written the Old Testament Scripture). Peter told how this Jesus had been ordained of God to be the judge of the quick and the dead, as well as to die and to rise from the dead. Peter told of his own experience of eating with Jesus after He rose from the dead, and of how Jesus had commanded him, and the others with him, to make all this known so that whosoever would believe in Him would receive remission of sins.

Even while Peter was still speaking, the Holy Spirit came upon those who believed. What astonished the Jews who were there, was that uncircumcised Gentiles could believe, receive the Holy Spirit, and be baptized even as they had been. They had felt that the wonder of being born again, (that which Jesus had explained to Nicodemus) was something that could happen only to Jews.

Now when the apostles and brethren that were in Judea heard that Gentiles had believed the word of God, they really were upset. When Peter returned to them in Jerusalem they argued with him quite fiercely: What did you go and talk and eat with a group of uncircumcised goys for? Their minds were full of criticism and disgust to think that Peter would eat with goys, not only eating nonkosher food, but identifying with them in the act of eating and talking.

Peter didn't just shout back some short reply like, "Keep quiet; I only did what God told me to." He carefully and patiently went over the entire story, so that they could have the same steps of explanation which convinced him. He told them so that they could really understand with their minds that God had opened the door to *other* nations, to people of the Gentiles, to come to Him through the Messiah, promised so long ago to the people of Israel. Peter knew they needed convincing. In spite of the fact that the promise to Abraham had been that the nations of the world would be blessed through his seed, the reality of that taking place was confusing to Jews who had always been accustomed to circumcision, the Day of Atonement, and the Passover being kept by *Jews* looking for their Messiah. It was a jolt to live in the very time when the door was suddenly wide open for *anyone* who would believe and accept this Messiah as his Savior.

Human beings show a selfishness and lack of compassion so often in history, and in their personal lives. It is so easy to want a cozy little relationship with other people, not to be penetrated by any stranger knocking at the gate! False lines of separation, and strange ghetto divisions, weird ideas of what makes one sort of group acceptable, and another sort to be relegated into another caste; standards which grow up among people who think they are wiping out segregation but are making a new kind of segregation: these things continue century after century. From the beginning God has had only two lines. Two lines from Cain and Abel on. Two lines made so clear by the two thieves on the two sides of Jesus when He was dying. There are only two kinds of people, those who believe God's Word, and those who do not.

The early church, the believing Jews, are now being shown very patiently and definitely that the division is *not* between Jew and Gentile, which division *they were in danger of making.*

FIFTEEN

Peter's story shows us very definitely that the Jews were the ones who were in danger of making the distinction between Jew and Gentile to be one of separation between believers in the Messiah and those who could not have any opportunity to believe.

How did the name "Christian" come to be used? What was it to distinguish? It was a name used first at Antioch, and the word was simply a rapid way of distinguishing between two sections of Jews, namely those who had come to be convinced that Jesus was the Old Testament-prophesied Messiah to which Moses pointed forward—and the Jews who denied this. "Christian" was a name given to Jews who had accepted Jesus Christ as the Messiah. The ones discussing these matters were all sitting together in synagogues listening to lectures and discussing. At times the arguments were hot, and the persecution was violent, but it had nothing to do with Gentile and Jew—all that has happened to put this connotation into the word "Christian" has been wrong, wrong, *wrong.*

It is a horrible thing that a man who believed *nothing* that God taught in His Word, a man named Hitler, should be synonymous with the word *Christian.* He was the very opposite of all that word means. In the first place, all the early Christians were Jews, and any *true* Christian should know the Old Testament well enough to know that he or she is one of the people Abraham's family was promised would be blessed through "the seed of Abraham." Understanding Christians should know they have been grafted in to the natural Olive tree. Understanding Christians should know that they are the spiritual seed of Abraham by being "born into the family" in the "new birth." Christians are *all* spiritual Jews.

There is a great need to clarify the use of the word *Christian.* If people want to make some ridiculous kind of segregated situation, the word *Christian* should be kept out of it.

A Gentile is anyone who is not a Jew. The word *Jew* distinguishes someone who is physically the seed of Abraham, no matter what passport he or she carries. The word *Gentile* applies to all others of every race and nation. There are atheistic, heathen, devil-worshiping, mystical, agnostic, liberal, humanistic—all kinds of religious and philosophic differences within *both* Jewish and Gentile camps. When you call a person a Jew or a Gentile, you have not necessarily said anything at all about his religion.

Christianity was first embraced by Jews because, as we have traced up to this point, it is the fulfillment of what had been promised and handed down by faithful Jews through the centuries, therefore it is far more Jewish than Gentile.

SIXTEEN

So if the word *Christian* only meant that Jews were labeling themselves or others as those who had accepted the fact of Christ being the Messiah, what did the word *church* mean? The early church simply was a gathering of Christians. The word had nothing to do with buildings. Since the first participants in the early church were Jews, it certainly was not anti-Jewish. If anything it was anti-Gentile, but gradually people learned that God meant the message of salvation through the Messiah, and everlasting life, to be given to any who would listen, regardless of their national, racial, religious, or philosophic background. The message was to be given to any who would listen. Peter's friends were astonished at all he told them, but their response finally was, "Then has God also to the Gentiles granted repentance unto life." We are told they were scattered abroad through persecution, Jew persecuting Jew, and traveled as far as Phoenice, Cyprus, and Antioch, preaching however only to other Jews.

After God initially used Peter to bring the message of the Messiah to the Gentiles, it was Paul who became the real missionary to the Gentiles as he went to Antioch in Syria, Iconium, Derbe, and Lystra. He also went to Corinth, Ephesus, Thessalonica, Rome, and perhaps even to Spain.

It is very interesting that Paul had strong messages to fit the need of both Jew and Gentile in the areas of their cultural background. In Antioch Paul was asked to speak in the

Synagogue on the Sabbath day, after the reading of the law and
the prophets. He gave them a "bird's-eye view" of the Old
Testament in a very condensed form as he started, "The God of
this people Israel chose our fathers, and exalted the people when
they dwelt as strangers in the land of Egypt, and with an high
arm brought he them out of it." Briefly summarizing
history, he comes up to the time of David and says, "Of this
man's seed hath God according to his promise raised unto Israel a
Savior, Jesus." He goes on after telling of John the Baptist:
"Men and brethren, children of the stock of Abraham, and
whosoever among you feareth God, to *you* is the word of this
salvation sent."

Paul tells of the life, death, and resurrection of this Jesus,
who he says is the one *through* whom forgiveness of sins can
be preached to them. "And by *him* all that believe are justified
from all things, from which ye could *not* be justified by the law of
Moses."

A fabulous thing happened, because when the Jews went
out of the Synagogue that day, the Gentiles begged that they
might hear this sermon or lecture preached to them the *next*
Sabbath, and many of the Jews followed Paul and Barnabas and
persuaded them to continue!

The next Sabbath almost the whole city came together to
hear the word of God. Now leading Jews were jealous of the
popularity of Paul and his message and spoke against what he
was saying. And Paul's reply was that it was necessary to
preach first to the Jews, but that if they didn't want to hear, he
would then turn to preaching to the Gentiles. The Gentiles heard
this and were glad and glorified God, and many believed and
were given eternal life. And the word of God was published
through all the region.

When Paul and Barnabas came to Iconium, we are told he again
taught right in the Synagogue of the Jews, and at that time
many believed, not only of Jews but of the Greeks. So the
early church is a place where the differences are being wiped
out. It is a drawing together of people who have before been
separated. When persecution broke out there against the
believers, the ones doing the stoning (Acts 14:5) were both

SIXTEEN

Gentiles and Jews. There was no division between Gentile and Jew that ticked off an assault—quite contrarily, Gentiles and Jews were Christians, and Gentiles and Jews were attacking the Christians.

The fact that differences were to be healed, to be wiped out, was stressed by Peter in answer to a group of men who came from Judea teaching that no one could be saved unless they had been circumcised as Moses taught. Also, a sect of Pharisees which now believed that Jesus was the Messiah taught in Jerusalem that it was necessary to circumcise any Gentile believers. Peter, who had been so well prepared by his experience with Cornelius, then makes something clear to them all in Acts 15:7, 9, 11: "Men and brethren," Peter says, "you know that a good while ago God chose that the Gentiles should hear the gospel and believe, by *my* speaking to them. And God put *no* difference between us and them, purifying their hearts by faith." So you see the point of Peter's explanation is that it *is* possible for Gentiles to become Christians without first becoming circumcised Jews. That was what had to be explained to the *Jews*. It took time for the concept to be understood that God had *sent* the Messiah, that He *had* died as the Lamb pointed forward to, and that now things were to be *different* in that *anyone* who would believe in Him would be redeemed without keeping a lot of ceremonial laws given to help people express the fact that they were waiting for the Messiah. Actually this perfectly fit what you will remember that God had promised Abraham in the first place. No longer is there a waiting for Him to come to redeem. Not only did Jews and Gentiles believe now, and find a relationship together that broke down former lines of division, but people of all walks of life believed—slave and master, household of Herod and peasant. Come to an amazing story of Paul and Silas in Philippi which was the chief city in that part of Macedonia. Right after Lydia, a seller of purple, had believed through their preaching, they were praying together, when a young girl came to speak to them, telling them she was possessed by an evil spirit and asking their help. Now this girl had brought a lot of money to men who used her as a fortune-teller, so when the spirit left her as Paul and Silas prayed, and she became a believer and felt calm and peaceful, the men became angry and trumped up a reason to have Paul and Silas thrown into prison for spoiling their source of money. The men who got them judged for their preaching were Romans who piously said, "They are teaching customs *we* are not lawfully allowed to observe, because *we* are Romans."

After being unfairly beaten and thrust into stocks, Paul and Silas were praying and singing praises to God, and the other prisoners heard them. Can't you imagine the mixed reactions? "Huh! what creeps—singing! What have they got to sing about?" some might have said. Others must have marveled and perhaps thought, "I wish I had something *real,* as they seem to have. What a reality *that* must be, which can't be blotted out by whipping and stocks."

Suddenly at midnight an earthquake shook the foundations of the prison (Acts 16:25-40) and all the doors opened. All the chains fell off the prisoners, and the stocks opened up. The keeper of the prison waked up out of a sound sleep and was terrified. When he saw doors wide open he drew out a sword to commit suicide, because he thought he would be blamed for the total escape of all his prisoners. But Paul shouted to him, "Don't harm yourself—we are all here." Then the keeper asked for a light, and came trembling to fall down before Paul and Silas, after which he led them out and asked one very serious question, "What must I do to be saved?"

This showed that the man had heard something of Paul and Silas's preaching, and had probably heard much arguing over what it was all about and whether it was truth or not. The man had this background of knowledge as well as having just experienced the supernatural earthquake and Paul and Silas's calmness not only in singing, but in not running away.

Their answer was, "Believe on the Lord Jesus Christ, and thou shalt be saved, and thy house." And then they *explained* the word of the Lord, which I am sure was a good, full "bird's-eye view" of Old Testament Scripture again, and the fulfillment which had taken place in the recent months, so that they could understand. It says, "They spake unto him the word of the Lord, and to all that were in his house," so it was like a Bible study for them all. The keeper of the prison did not forget to wash Paul and Silas and put something on their bruises, and after that we are told that he was baptized and so were all his family—"straightway." What a scene we see as our "bird" swoops down on this part of Bible history! Prisoners and head guard with all his family, now sitting, eating and laughing, rejoicing *together* over the marvel of truth, and believing together in what God had made so clear to them all. Now prisoner and keeper are together, the line of difference wiped out. What a healing thing God has given when He has said we can be "one people" in what Christ came to do!

When they left the prison the next day after seeing the magistrates (who, by the way, got scared when they found Paul had a Roman citizenship), they went right away to Lydia's house where they comforted the believers gathered there, who had been frightened by all that had taken place.

Next we find them preaching and discussing in a Synagogue again, this time in Thessalonica. We are told that in this Synagogue Paul took three Sabbath days to make things plain and to reason with the Jews "out of the Scriptures." The "Scriptures" refer always to the Old Testament, as the New had not yet been written, so what Paul does for the Jews is to go over the history, the prophecy, giving a "bird's-eye view" *sufficient* for the people to be convinced that the present moment of history "fit in" and that prophecy had really been fulfilled. We are told that in Thessalonica "some of them believed, and consorted with Paul and Silas." That would be Jews being spoken of. "And of the devout Greeks a great multitude, and of the chief women not a few." So lots of Jews, Greeks, and leading women became Christians in Thessalonica.

The uproar of persecution was to follow like thunder and lightning on a clear summer's day. The opposition is always fierce. Why? Because God's Word, whether to Eve and Adam, Cain and Abel, Noah and his family, Abraham and his family, Moses and Aaron, Joshua, Esther, Jeremiah, Isaac, or the days of Jesus preaching, or Peter, Paul and Silas, or our own time of history—God's Word given at *any* time of history is *truth* being opposed by Satan the liar, who hates truth. Satan stirs up men to hate that which cuts across the things which they have succumbed to, in believing his lies. Satan *hates* the continuity of true truth.

If there *is no truth,* and there are no lies—if there are no absolutes, and there is no such thing as right and wrong—then there could *be* no opposition. If everything is relative, and no fixed truth exists but a fluid situation which is in flux, then how could there be opposition? What would it matter what people believed? What possible difference would it make? It could then make no difference to the people believing something, nor to the people *not* believing.

In Athens Paul was stirred up by seeing a whole city given to idolatry, worshiping a great variety of idols and gods of men's imaginations. These men were philosophers but they included many possible gods to worship and for good measure had an altar where they could worship "The Unknown God." Paul was so compassionate in his concern for these men that he went from where he had been discussing and teaching Jews in the Synagogue in Athens, and stood on Mars Hill to speak to the Greeks. What a great speech it was, that one on Mars Hill. Happily, some of it has been preserved for us.

Paul cleverly began: "Ye men of Athens, I perceive that in all things you are too superstitious. I was passing by during your devotions, and I saw an altar with this inscription, 'To the Unknown God.' This one whom ye *ignorantly* worship, I will now declare unto you." Paul then went on to tell that God had made the world and everything in it, as He is the God of heaven and of earth, giving life and breath to all things. He stressed that all nations had originally been made of one blood. He gave that which he could have sung, had Handel already written it—something on the order of "If with all your hearts ye truly seek Him, ye shall ever surely find Him"—which, of course, we have already quoted out of the Old Testament. Paul put it this way: "God ... made of one blood all nations of men to dwell on the earth,... that they should *seek* the Lord ... and find him, though he be not far from everyone of us: for in *him* we live, and move and have our being...." Then he went on to tell of the coming time of judgment by Jesus, "the man whom he hath ordained," who had been raised from the dead (Acts 17:22-34). When they heard about the resurrection some mocked him, and others said they wanted to hear more, and *some* believed. Two are named, a man named Dionysius and a woman named Damaris, but there were others.

So you see there were Greeks now, being added to other Gentiles who believed, although the very core of the early church is Jewish. Paul, who had been trained from boyhood by Jewish parents, became a "child of the Law" at thirteen and was brought to Jerusalem to be taught by Gamaliel (the grandson of the brilliant Hillel). Paul then had a fantastic training sitting at the feet of such a teacher, and knew the Old Testament Scriptures inside out! This well trained Paul, who first persecuted Christians, became the greatest of the apostles in intellect and influence—among Jews and also Gentiles. Paul was the missionary who traveled far and wide, as well as being the one who wrote many of the Epistles in the New Testament. He was prisoner in Rome in his own house for two years, and during that time he talked to many who came to him, as well as to the guards. Wherever he was, people came to *know* something of truth, because his explanations were so full, and always based on the Scriptures which he knew well, and which he realized so marvelously had been fulfilled in what Christ had done.

The greatest missionary of all time is what Paul is often called, and that means that the greatest missionary of the Christian church was a Jew. It was this Jew who opened the way for Gentiles to understand.

Our bird seems to be a hummingbird at this moment, almost standing still, hovering over a honeysuckle flower, at the time of the early church. We must fly on or we won't have the complete view, even from the air! It is impossible to spend too much time at any one point.

However, there are a few necessary places to pause before going to the picture we are giving in the book of Revelation of the future time ahead.

We must know that it is possible to read Paul's writings in the Epistles as well as to study some of his other speeches and sermons in the book of Acts. We must stop to think how staggering a proof it is of the reasonableness of Christ's being the One who fulfilled all the prophecies of the Messiah, when such a brilliant and educated man as Paul was so intellectually convinced, and also willing to defend—to the very end—the things he believed to be true. For Paul was in the end martyred, and so will be one of the martyrs who will receive the special "martyr's crown" spoken of later in the Bible. Paul's courage to stand before Jews, Greeks, and Romans was fantastic. Paul himself said that he was ready to go to Rome, "For I am not ashamed of the gospel of Christ: for it is the power of God unto salvation to every one that believeth, to the Jew first and also to the Greek." In the book of Romans we see how he spoke to people who had no background of having read the Old Testament Scriptures, *and* to those who knew the Scriptures very well. He makes very clear that it was not circumcision which saved Abraham, but that the circumcision was simply a seal to show he had already believed. Speaking of Abraham, Paul said, "He staggered not at the promise of God through unbelief; but was strong in faith, giving glory to God; and being fully persuaded that what he had promised he was able also to perform ... therefore it was imputed to him for righteousness" (Romans 4:20, 21, 22). "Oh, Jews," Paul is saying, "all this was not written for Abraham's sake alone, but for us also, because this same righteousness will be imputed to us, if we believe on him who raised up Jesus our Lord from the dead. Who [that is, Jesus] was delivered up to die for our sin, and was raised up again from the dead for our justification."

Paul made things crystal clear to Jews and Gentiles, and God had him write these inspired things so that for centuries, right up until the time Jesus comes back, there will be no lack of information in order that the seeking ones may come to understand, and have eternal life.

Paul did not speak without going back to Adam in *his* "bird's-eye view," for instance when he said that "by one man's disobedience many were made sinners, so by the obedience of one, shall many be made righteousness." The continuity is there. The threads are woven together in the whole Bible in a marvelously beautiful tapestry, and when people begin removing threads which they don't like, other parts of the tapestry ravel, and they end up with ugly holes which cannot be mended. Liberal theologians destroy their *own* understanding as they cut out historic things from the books of Moses, because the Jews who believed in the days of the early church understood the continuity and naturally talked about it, as well as being inspired by God to show that the warp and woof of His teaching through all history makes one whole piece of cloth.

Dear Paul! Before we leave him we must stand beside him for a moment, remembering Joseph as he wept over his brothers who had been so mean to him, remembering Christ as He wept over Jerusalem as so many rejected Him, and hear in Romans 9 Paul's cry that demonstrates the same compassion: "I have great heaviness and continual sorrow in my heart. For I could wish that I myself were accursed from Christ for my brethren, my kinsmen according to the flesh who are Israelites." He goes on in chapter 10 to say that his "heart's desire and prayer to God for Israel is, that they might be saved." His prayer was for the Israeli people living at that moment of history ... but also for their children and grandchildren down through the years. Paul, who was the missionary to the Gentiles and who taught thoroughly that all who believe become *one* in God's family, nevertheless agonized over the people of his *own* flesh. Paul would have been astonished if anyone had told him that Christianity was to be a dividing word between Jew and Gentile. Paul knew Christianity was Jewish, and that it was a very great thing that the door had been opened to Gentiles too.

Christianity was meant to be a binding word, to bind together Jew and Gentile. It has done this throughout history in some people's lives, and it did so in the beginning. But the word *Christian* was to be stolen, to be used as a synonym for "civilized," or for "goodness," or for some other quality in people who might, as far as belief in God goes, be atheists. Then it was also stolen to be used as a word dividing Gentile from Jew, and it was to be plastered up on advertising folders, or spit out as a blasphemy because of its very opposite connotation.

To go back to Paul as he stands in front of the Romans, hover on bird's wings to listen as he so beautifully speaks: "... the scripture says, Whosoever believeth on him [that is the Messiah, Jesus] shall not be ashamed. For there is no difference between the Jew and the Greek: for the *same* Lord over all is rich unto *all* that call upon him. For whosoever shall call upon the name of the Lord shall be saved." It is right at this point that Paul stresses the need to *know* the content of the teaching of the Word of God. He says no one can believe who hasn't heard, and that people won't hear unless someone tells them. However, he then goes back through the Bible and says that Moses made it known, and that Isaiah also made things clear, and that when Elijah had his confrontation there were 7000 who believed. Paul goes through the "remnant" of believers whom we have followed in this book, and he says, "Even so at this present time there is *also* a remnant ..." as, of course, many were believing right then.

Now we come to the place I spoke about to those Jewish men in New York, when I stood on the soap box, for we come to Romans 11 where Paul pleads with the Gentiles who have believed to recognize that they have been grafted into the tree. And that the Jews who were cut off because they did not believe, can also change and believe and be grafted back in. Paul prophesies here that a time is coming when many, *many* Jews will come back to the God of Abraham through the Messiah.

You see how it is all woven together? The door is open for Gentiles to come in. The Shepherd takes lambs into the fold which are not Jewish. The Tree has wild branches grafted in which will bear fruit because the same roots are there. The family is to be *one.* Paul quotes Isaiah 11:10 when he says, "There shall be a root of Jesse and he that shall rise to reign over the Gentiles; in *him* shall the Gentiles trust." Which is another prophecy of that which the Messiah will do.

Paul "wraps it up" in his letter to the Galatians, when he says: "For you are all the children of God by faith in Christ Jesus ... there is neither Jew nor Greek, there is neither bond nor

free, there is neither male nor female: for you are all one in
Christ Jesus. And if ye be Christ's then are ye *Abraham's
seed,* and heirs according to the promise."

What a staggering statement! If it is true, then it is the most
integrating principle possible. How fantastic! Has it been
demonstrated throughout the last twenty centuries by every
believer and all believing groups? Unhappily, no. Men have
failed to demonstrate the truth which they have claimed to
believe. Again it is a picture of the cruelty of man to man.

What does Paul's statement in Galatians 3:28, 29 mean?
It means that there is not meant to be any division between
Jewish and Gentile people who have believed in the Messiah.
One is not to be superior to the other. There is not to be any
division economically between people—no caste system of
slaves and masters, they are to be equal, as they are in the same
family and "born" with the same birth! No claim to "better blood"
is to be found among children of the living God who all have
experienced the "new birth," the "second birth" which now
wipes out the effects of the first birth in a very real way. You
can't be born in a ghetto in the second birth; you can't be born in a
high or low caste ... we are all of one birth. And if you belong
to Christ, says Paul with the inspiration God gave him
because this is God's message to us, then you are *"Abraham's
seed."* What? This means that very specifically *every* Christian is a
spiritual seed of Abraham, Jew and Gentile alike. Spiritually
we *all* come from the *same* father on *earth,* as well as having
the same Heavenly Father. We are Abraham's seed.

Amazing? But that is what God says. When we experience the
second birth, by believing inwardly—not by "joining a
party"—we become of "one blood," all following Abraham
as far as our earthly status goes, and of one family in which we
are "heirs" along with Christ. God is also our Father.

Paul goes on to say that we all are in the place of Isaac: we are
children of promise. We are the rightful children of God,
through the Messiah, the one and only way we *could* become
His children. It all ties in, you see.

Paul, as he preaches these facts to the Gentiles in Ephesians,
says he was willing to be a *prisoner* and to suffer *all* sorts of

things so that they could *know.* Don't worry about all the tribulations I have had to go through, he says. "For this cause I bow my knees unto the Father of our Lord Jesus Christ, of whom the *whole family in heaven and earth is named."*

Thank God, in this day of broken nations, broken promises by government leaders, broken hopes, broken relationships on every level from the family to the races, that *there is a family which is one,* and that is the family God has made it possible to gather together with all differences ironed out.

> *How odd of God*
> *To choose the Jew;*
> *But not so odd*
> *As those who choose*
> *The Jewish God*
> *And hate the Jew.*

The Jew who becomes a Christian should be more aware and excited about her or his Jewish heritage than ever before because he has become a fulfilled Jew, or a Bible-believing Jew, really believing the Old Testament and then all that is clearly fulfilled in the New Testament. The Gentile who has become a Christian should be aware that he or she now is a spiritual seed of Abraham and that all the Jewish heritage belongs in a thrilling way to him or to her as the Old Testament is believed as well as the fulfillment in the New Testament.

From what source, then, can anti-Semitism come? From what source can anti-*any* group come? From what source can pride in "blood" or "race" or social background, or economic background, or any of the ugly dividing things come? Where did ghettos originate? Who is behind it all? Certainly not God, and not any who correctly believe Him and follow His teaching. The original "oneness" was spoiled when Satan tempted Eve and Adam with his lies which brought about separation. The source of all separation is *anti-God.*

There will come the culmination of all this one day on the earth in a man who will be the *Anti-*Christ.

The anti-Semitics, as well as anti- other peoples, are really anti-God.

SEVENTEEN

There is only one kind of separation which God makes clear took place when Eve and Adam chose to believe Satan rather than God's specific verbalized explanation of cause and effect. The separation which has continued all through history is the separation caused by man believing Satan rather than God. Cain's sacrifice made this pointedly vivid to any who want understanding. There are those at any point in history who have come to God, as Abel did, Abraham did, Moses did, Joseph did, Isaiah did, with the lamb. There are those who believed, as we have seen, that the Lamb of God did come and die, and who accepted Him when He was still on earth, and there are those who look back, believing the truth of all this history and accepting what has been done for them by the Lamb of God.

The necessary thing that has to take place, to assure us that we are in the "stream" of believers, on Abel's line, definitely spiritual seed of Abraham, is really very simple. It does not cost any silver or gold, nor does it require special degrees or intellectual status. A child can understand all that it is necessary to know as a "base" for assurance that one is now on the right line, counted among the spiritual seed of Abraham.

There is the need to believe God is *there.* "He that cometh to God must believe that He *is,* and that He is the rewarder of them that diligently seek Him." Yes, there is a need to believe that God, the God of creation, the God of the Old Testament, the God of Abraham, Isaac, and Jacob, the God of Peter and Paul,

the God of the whole Bible, really exists and that he is
personal—Father, Son, and Holy Spirit.

Then there is the need to understand something of the reality
of guilt before a Holy God in having broken not only His clear
Ten Commandments but even our own standards, and to
realize that one has sinned, and that this sin needs atonement.

There is also need to recognize with some measure of
understanding that God has been totally fair in showing
throughout the centuries the *way* to atone, with constantly
increased detail being given, but never a change in the *way*.
There is a need to recognize the true truth of all that Peter, Paul,
and others have given in the "bird's-eye view" of the whole
Bible's teaching, and to realize that this is history. This
means coming to believe that what has been given in God's
Word is historical truth, not just a vague religious truth. It means
believing what Mary knew to be true, that the Messiah was
virgin born, that indeed as John said, "In the beginning was
the Word ... and the Word became flesh...." That it was God
the Son, the Second Person of the Trinity, who came to walk up
that hill that central day in all history, when He could expect no
substitute, no miracle to remove Him from suffering and
death, because He Himself was the only One who could be the
atonement, the substitute, *The Lamb.*

Finally there is the need to bow before the living God, and
acknowledge that no possible thing that we could bring in
our hands would balance, wipe out, or atone for our sins, and
accept what He has done for us as the atonement *needed.* There is
need to bow, and to accept what the Messiah has done as a free
gift. Peter in his first Epistle, 1 Peter 1:17-20, puts it very
clearly: "And if ye call on the Father, who without respect of
persons judgeth according to every man's work, pass the time of
your sojourning here in fear: Forasmuch as ye know that ye
were not redeemed with corruptible things, as silver and
gold, from your vain conversation received by tradition from
your fathers: but with the *precious blood of Christ, as of a Lamb
without blemish and without spot:* Who verily *was* foreordained
before the foundation of the world, but was manifest in
these last times *for you.* Who by him do believe in God, that

194

raised him up from the dead, and gave him glory; that your faith and hope might be in God."

Then Peter gives a solemn warning: "For all flesh is as grass, and all the glory of man as the flower of grass. The grass withereth, and the flower thereof falleth away: but the word of the Lord endureth forever. And *this is the word* which by the gospel is preached unto you."

Anyone who believes His Word, and accepts the provision which He made for atonement, is immediately born again—is now a spiritual seed of Abraham, and has his feet firmly fixed on the "line" springing from Abel.

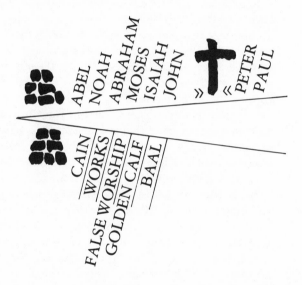

Anyone who is born a second time, who has gone through "the new birth," now has everlasting life. There is a future, and God has given us some small glimpses of what that future will include.

Perhaps questions come to our minds in the continuity of the flow, as to some of the transitions from things which needed to be done in the B.C. days, which are different now in the A.D. days! Our calendars tell us there is a difference and we date our letters, acknowledging the central moment in history, but what changes did God teach through the writers of the New Testament?

Where are the priests of the Old Testament times? The priests were to be go-betweens—they were mediators between God and men. The priests brought the sacrifice, put their hands on the head of the animal, and said something like this, "This lamb has done nothing, but may the sins of this person be placed upon this lamb." The High Priest went once a year into the holy of holies to bring the blood of the lamb for *all* the people.

Remember that when Jesus was dying, He was the Priest Himself, as well as The Lamb? Remember that the veil in the Temple was torn in two pieces? In the book of Hebrews we are told that the priests went daily into the tabernacle to sacrifice, but that into the second place, the holy of holies where the ark was, "went the high priest once a year alone, not without blood, which he offered for himself and for the errors of the people." Then we read, "But Christ being come an high priest of good things to come, by a greater and more perfect tabernacle ... neither by the blood of goats and calves, but by his *own blood* he entered in once, into the Holy Place, having obtained eternal redemption for us."

So the Messiah, Christ, *is* the High Priest, and will be forever. He intercedes for us. We are told that now He is on the right hand of the Father interceding for us. He prays for the ones who have come to believe and accept Him, and He pleads His own blood, saying, "I died for this person, forgive this person, hear the prayer of this one...." He is the *only* High Priest we need, the One who is also our Lamb.

Are there to be any other priests? Peter says in his first Epistle, "Ye are a chosen generation, a royal priesthood, an holy nation, a peculiar people, that you should show forth the praises of *him* who called you out of darkness into *his* marvelous light." Peter is saying that every believer is now a priest. Every believer can intercede for the other people who are not believers. It is a great responsibility to be a priest! It means not some special robes or status, it simply means entrance into the presence of God—possible day and night at any moment, because of what the Messiah did for us. Jesus opened the way back into that communication which was broken between God and people when Eve and Adam sinned. Now day by day we can walk and talk with God.

Paul says in his letter to Timothy, 1 Timothy 1:1-6, that he strongly urges supplications, prayers, intercession, and giving of thanks to be made for all men; for kings and all in authority, because God wants us to be praying and interceding in order that men might come to have knowledge of *the truth*.

So now all who believe and have therefore been born again, are in the place of "priests," and have a responsibility to pray for the rest of the people. It is a terrible thing to turn away from this responsibility—it is a cruelty to those for whom we are the only priests.

Were there to be no people to spend a special amount of time studying the Word of God, praying, and answering people's questions, teaching and giving sacraments? Yes, "elders" are spoken of as leading the early church in the book of Acts, and the requirements for elders are given in the book of Titus. Elders are to be spiritual men, born again, of course, and given to prayer and study of the Bible. They are to be the husband of one wife, men who rule their children well. There was no command that every elder *must* marry, as Paul specifically said some would have a special gift of God not to need to marry, but there was no command for elders, deacons, and evangelists *not* to marry. In other words, as they are leaders in the family of God, they need to be men who lead their own families well, and understand family life. There were preaching elders, and those who ruled—a kind of committee. When the discussion of carrying out the admonition to care for the widows and children came up, then deacons were appointed to take care of gathering funds and sharing this money with the poor and specially needy people. We are told that Christians are supposed to take care of each other, and not to allow huge financial differences to grow up, and the deacons were supposed to facilitate this distribution, being sensitive to the fact that there were people in need, and seeing that others shared.

Elders were to study to be able to teach the true truth to
people, and to answer questions and be a spiritual help. The
word "minister" is another word that was used, with the basic
meaning of "ministering to people's needs."

What were the sacraments that these Elders or ministers
were to administer? There would no longer be a day of
atonement, because *The* Day of Atonement had taken place
when The Lamb died, at the passover time. What would take the
place of the Day of Atonement and the passover feast? Jesus
himself began that *with* the disciples as He ate with them
the Last Supper or the Last Passover. He told them that from
that time on they would eat the bread and drink the wine, looking
forward to His second coming, and back to His death.

Paul explained it to the Corinthian church in 1 Corinthians
11:23-27. He said that Jesus, in the very same night when He
was to be betrayed, took bread, "And when he had given
thanks he broke it, and said, Take, eat, this is my body which is
broken for you: this do ye in *remembrance* of me. After the same
manner also he took the cup, and when he had supped he said,
This cup is the new testament in my blood: this do ye as oft
as ye drink it, in remembrance of me. For as often as you eat
this bread and drink this cup, ye do show the Lord's death until he
come."

You see the Passover was to be celebrated from the time
of Moses, until the death of the firstborn Son of God, who
would take the place of *all* who would come to Him. After His
death, then there was no need to look back to the Passover in
Egypt, because there is now a need to look *back* to the
Messiah's death, and *ahead to the Messiah's second coming.*
Communion, although very ignorantly taken by many people, is
meant to be an understanding on the part of believers that they
are remembering that Jesus' body was broken for them, and
His blood was shed for them, and that *one day* He is really
coming back again, in space, and time, and history—in the future
history. It is not a mystical ceremony to give people some
vague religious feeling. In fact Paul warns that people can
drink it unworthily, and that that is a damnation. In other
words, if people do not *believe,* and simply take communion as a

religious gobbledegook of mysticism, it is less than a help to them, it is a condemnation. The reality of believing these things are true is more important than the outward expression, and an empty, hollow, unbelieving expression of an outward sort is the *living* of a lie!

It's just as it was in the Old Testament times, when people were told that it was "the circumcision of the heart" that counted! What did that mean? It meant that the inward belief was what made a person the spiritual seed of Abraham, way back in those days. The reality of believing that God is there and that He speaks truth, is what counts—not just outward practices, whether A.D. or B.C.!

Circumcision was the sign given in the body of all the boy babies, that they were part of the family of Israel, and that their parents were promising to teach them all they needed to know and believe about God. Any male person becoming a part of Israel from a heathen nation was then circumcised, and his babies were circumcised. And a woman who became Jewish, as Rahab did, then had her boy babies circumcised. However after Jesus died, and the Jews now had their Messiah, the door was open to the Gentiles too.

Remember that we have been told that now there is no male or female, as well as that there is no Jew or Gentile? There is a sign to be given which will include all people, and wipe out the differences. Baptism takes the place of circumcision. Baptism is for female and male, for Jew and Gentile—to show that each one now is living at the marvelous moment of history which gives us a place in the *new covenant.* Jesus has died, Jesus is coming back again, and now people are to have the opportunity of all being in the same family with God as their Father, and with Abraham as their spiritual father, and girls as well as boys can have the sign of this being true, as well as Jews and Gentiles.

Worship now is to be on the day Jesus arose, commemorating the wonder of His resurrection. We look forward to the time when the *last* enemy will be conquered, and the last enemy is death. There is a day coming when there will be no more death. So as we look back to Jesus' resurrection, we look forward to our own resurrection, when our bodies will be changed to be like His glorious body. He gave us the "proof" to remember, Sunday by Sunday, as we remember the reality of the resurrection, so carefully attested to during those forty days. Hallelujah, Christ arose—the Messiah is not a dead Messiah, but a living One, and He promises us everlasting life in changed bodies, resurrected bodies. The work of redemption was finished when Christ arose.

In Hebrews 11:13 the writer tells us that all those who believed, like Abel, Enoch, Noah, Abraham and so on, saw the promises "afar off" and they "confessed that they were pilgrims and strangers on earth"; "But now they desire a better country, that is an heavenly; wherefore God is *not ashamed* to be called their God: for he hath prepared for them a city."

What is this talking about—that God is not ashamed to be called their God? The chapter goes on to tell of fantastic things that came about through the faith of such people as Isaac, Jacob, and Moses. It tells about kingdoms being subdued, lions' mouths being stopped, enemies being defeated—marvelous answers to prayer. Of course God would not be ashamed to be called their God. But wait; later on the chapter speaks of people being persecuted, being beaten and mocked, being stoned and cut in half, having all sorts of difficulties. What about these people? Their neighbors and friends very likely have said, "What a God they have! Why does He let them suffer so much—all that cancer, loss of bank account in the depression, sons dying at war—what a God can that be?" But God says He is not ashamed to be called the God of His children, because He has prepared for them a city. Jesus said, "I go to prepare a place for you, and if I go I will come again and take you to be with me. In my Father's house there are many mansions, (or rooms)" He says—and this is a specific promise, "That where I am there you may be forever."

Promises by God will be kept. He made a covenant with Abraham and it was kept. He has made a new covenant, and it will all be kept. We have been promised that when we are in His family, He will comfort us when we need comfort. Comfort? That means we will have sorrow. He has said He will

give strength in our weakness, when we ask Him. His strength
to be given us in our weakness, means we are to expect to
feel weak, many times. He says He will give us victory when we
are attacked. Yes, God promises His children guidance, His
wisdom, comfort, strength, victory, all kinds of help, but He
does *not* promise them an easy life in this world. It is when
the Messiah comes back again that things will change. There
will be reality now. There will be reality of communication with
Him, and His answers. There will be reality of knowing His
comfort and strength. But there will not be perfection, and
all troubles will not be immediately taken away. Satan
continues to do as he did to Job so long ago: he tries to cut off
communication and trust so that the people of God will stop
loving their Father. There is a battle which started in heaven
with Lucifer, which is still going on.

Paul is very, very strong in letting people know about this. Paul,
that marvelous Jew, that wonderful missionary to the Gentiles,
the one who knew the Old Testament so very well, makes
brilliantly clear the fact that we are not to expect an easy life.
He tells of his own troubles, in his second letter to the church at
Corinth. After he says, "Are they Hebrews? so am I. Are they
Israelites? so am I," he goes on to say, "Are they ministers of
Christ? so am I, in labors more abundant, in stripes above
measure, in prisons more frequent ... of the Jews five times I
received thirty-nine stripes, three times I was beaten with rods,
once I was stoned, three times I was shipwrecked, a whole
day and night in water. I have been in journeys often, in perils
of waters, of robbers, in perils by my own countrymen, in perils by
the heathen, in perils in the city, in perils in the wilderness, in
perils among false brethren. In weariness and painfulness,
in watchings often in cold and nakedness ..." (2 Cor.
11:23-27). Paul then goes on to say that in addition to all these
things, he had a "thorn in the flesh," something which was
physical which troubled him. Was he healed? No. He asked
the Lord three times to take this away, and the answer that
came was this: "My grace is sufficient for thee: for my strength is
made perfect in weakness."

There *will* be marvelous answers to prayer in this life.

God is able to do "the impossible" for His children. But there are two kinds of answers! Paul did not have *in*sufficient faith, simply there was a need of an answer of giving him sufficient *"grace"* to live with that horrible thorn in the flesh and still love and trust God as a demonstration that that grace was indeed *real.* The other kind of answer is the supply of what has been asked for—in other words, an affirmative answer to prayer.

It is because death is an enemy, death is not natural, death is a separation, that Jesus came to die, so that we could have life, and have it forever. This period of time is only temporary for those who are born twice, because the second birth is a forever and ever birth. Paul puts it this way to the Galatians: "And because ye are sons, God has sent forth the Spirit of his Son into your hearts, crying, Abba, Father. Wherefore you are no more a servant, but a son; and if a son, then an heir of God through Christ" (Galatians 4:6, 7).

We have much which we are inheriting. And in our bird's flight through the Bible we must dip down to have glimpses of the future prophecy which gives us some idea of the wonders in store for us.

But while we believers are waiting for that fantastic moment to happen, we are supposed to be not only praying for the others who do not yet know, not only telling others who do not know, but demonstrating something of a reality of now being closer to what man was supposed to be in the first place. With the help of the Holy Spirit, with the help of the intercession of Jesus, with the help of the Father who hears as we cry out to Him, we are meant to be concerned about being "different." So lying, filthy communication, blasphemy, anger, malice, so Paul says, ought to be put aside, and "Put on the new man," he says, "which is renewed in the image of him that created him: Where there is neither Greek nor Jew, circumcision nor uncircumcision, barbarian, Scythian, bond or free." Put on therefore, as you are now children of the living God, some of the qualities that show you are made in His image. The ones mentioned are "mercy, kindness, humbleness, meekness, longsuffering, forgiving one another, and love." These things are to mark the difference in people who are *back* in the family of God. In one place we are told that the greatest mark of the difference, is *love* (Colossians 3:8-14).

We are not to be looking for annihilation of the earth as the next event in history, because we are told we are to look for the second coming of Christ. We are to comfort one another with reminding each other that He *is* coming again. "For the Lord himself shall descend from heaven with a shout, with the voice of the archangel, and with the trump of God: and the dead in Christ [who died believing in the Old Testament days looking forward, at the time of the Messiah, or afterwards] shall rise first: Then we which are alive and remain shall be caught up together with them in the air: and so shall we ever be with the Lord. Wherefore comfort one another with these words."

Does it mean we don't *care* about the atomic bombs? Does it mean that we don't *care* about bombs in tunnels and riots in the streets? Does it mean we don't *care* about ecological imbalances endangering our food supply? Does it mean we don't *care* about depression? No, there are things for us to *do* now as we ask God for guidance and help to be used by Him *in* this moment of history. But we are not to panic. We are not to feel that life has no meaning. We are not to feel insignificant in a machine universe. We are not to give up and commit suicide. There is a purpose now, and there is a future coming in which there will be perfection.

Jesus is coming back, and the promises to Abraham are to have their complete fulfillment. The Messiah who was to be a suffering Messiah, was also to be King, and His coming in power and great glory is ahead for both Jews and Gentiles. The detail of fulfillment of His first coming is an example of how detail-perfect His second coming will be.

Paul warns us in 1 Thessalonians 5:4-6: "But ye brethren are not in darkness that that day should overtake you as a thief. You are all the children of light, and the children of the day: we are not of the night, nor of darkness. Therefore, let us not sleep as do others, but let us watch...!" And verse 24: "Faithful is he that calleth you, who also will *do* it."

We have evidence enough through the centuries that the God of Abraham, Moses, David, Isaiah, Paul, is *there,* and that *His Word is trustworthy.*

What has He promised us? Peter tells us in 2 Peter 3:13: "According to his promise, we look for new heavens and a new earth, wherein dwelleth righteousness."

EIGHTEEN

As our bird's flight through the Bible takes us to places in the final book, Revelation, we can only touch down at a few spots. This last book is an exciting finale to all that God has given us to know before we are with Him and see things "face to face." We are given something of the wonder and glory that is ahead when the final victory is won, and we enter into an eternity in our resurrected bodies. Ezekiel in the Old Testament gave some of this too.

John, the Apostle and evangelist, wrote Revelation, having been given the visions and inspiration which gave him what God would have him write, on the Greek island Patmos—a rocky spot in the Grecian archipelago, southwest of Ephesus. When one contemplates the terrible things which had taken place in John's lifetime, such as the reign of Nero and the horrible persecutions, the destruction of the Temple and the devastation of Jerusalem in Titus's time, the "backdrop" of discouragement and defeat would make a dark background indeed on which to be shown the marvel of what was ahead. What a comfort the content of Revelation must have been to John himself as first of all he saw it, and then wrote it down for the encouragement of all who would read it, believing. If this future "history" is true, then we have a bright future which present blackness cannot blot out. For those who do believe it *is* true, then the comparison to the perfect fulfillment of Christ's first coming is a certainty that causes us to expect detailed fulfillment of the events described. However, always in looking forward to something prophesied, one's understanding cannot be perfect. Some day we shall say, "Oh, now I see—of course!" But even with imperfect understanding, there is a certainty that it all fits together with the whole of the Scriptures. We have not come to that which has no base in history, the threads are still there which we have been following all the way through.

We still recognize that Christianity is Jewish as we dip down into various places in the Apocalypse, or Revelation.

The One who John says will come with the clouds, "and every eye shall see him and they which pierced him: and all kindreds of the earth shall wail because of him," is no other one than the Lamb, who is also "Alpha and Omega, the beginning and the end, the Lord which is and which was and which is to come, the Almighty."

This One now appears to John on the island of Patmos, in marvelous glistening glory so that the sight was too much for John and he fell to his face before Him. Jesus tenderly leans down and puts His hand on John, saying, "Don't be afraid, I am the first and the last. I am the living one who became dead, and behold I am alive forevermore, Amen." John is being given certainty that indeed this is the Lord with whom he has walked and talked in the years before, whose tomb he examined right after the resurrection, who appeared in the upper room when he was there, with whom he ate fish and honeycomb. This same Jesus, whom John loves and serves, is now commissioning John to do a task which he must have thought was really "too much" for him. He does not have to do it in his own strength, nor by his own knowledge or imagination—he is going to be given a view, and given inspiration through which he will know what God wants him to know in writing a description accurately for everyone who would be reading this in their seeking and studying the truth.

"Write the things which thou hast seen, and the things which are, and the things which shall be hereafter."

John is given messages to give to the churches then existing, but messages which it is important for churches to study and

EIGHTEEN

understand, and apply to themselves today. Then we are told,
"After this I looked, and behold, a door was opened in heaven,
and the first voice which I heard was as it were of a trumpet
talking with me; which said, Come up hither and I will show
you things which must be hereafter."

A marvelous voice as clear as a trumpet ... inviting John to see
things which are coming, so that he can give us a glimpse of
some of them. Can we know "perfectly"? No, because we
are not ready to understand it perfectly, but we can know as
much as God meant us to know of some of the details that are
ahead.

God did not have this written to mean "nothing" to us;
He gave it to mean "something." As we fly as a bird with John
that day, let us swoop down at some special places. Let us see the
amazing way that the *Lamb* is prominent in the time ahead. We
can have absolutely no doubt as we follow the Lamb, that we
are being told that from Abel's lamb on through the centuries,
there is only *one* Person being represented by the lamb.

In Revelation 5 we are told of a book that has seven seals, and
no man can be found in the universe who is worthy to open
this special book or to look at it. Then one of the twenty-four
elders says, "Don't weep, there is someone, who is the Lion of the
tribe of Judah, the Root of David ... he can open the seals!" In
case this one being described is not recognized, we are then
told that John saw in the midst of the elders a Lamb—standing.
It had been slain but it is now standing. This one came and took
the book and opened it, and the elders fell down before the
Lamb and worshiped with a marvelous song. We are given
the words of this song, which is called a *new* song. What
gorgeous music it must have been set to as the words rolled out
into John's ears. One day we are to hear it and thrill:

"Thou art worthy to take the book and to open the seals
thereof: for thou wast slain, and hast redeemed us to God by
thy blood out of every kindred, and tongue, and people, and
nation: and hast made us unto our God kings and priests: and
we shall reign on the earth."

How thrillingly tied together with all we have seen from the
Old and New Testaments is this song! The song is of praise to the

Messiah who was slain, killed to provide redemption for both Jew and Gentile out of every family line, every language group, every kind of people and nation. These redeemed ones have been "priests" as we saw in our last chapter, and there *will* be a time when they will "reign" on the earth when Jesus comes back. The song is a gorgeous tie-up of past history, present, and of what is coming. Then John heard a rising volume of voices as angels began to say the same thing with one accord, all with loud voices. John says he saw them around the throne, "ten thousand times ten thousand, and thousands of thousands." Are you a mathematician? That is a lot of angels. And what are they saying with their loud angelic voices? "Worthy is the *Lamb* that was slain, to receive power, and riches, and wisdom, and strength, and honor, and glory and blessing."

No longer is the Lamb being spit upon and hit on every side. No longer is the Lamb hanging upon the cross in naked shame. Now He is in His glory, having redeemed the people for whom He died, and the angels are shouting with deep, understanding appreciation of all He suffered, with great joy that He accomplished the work of redemption, that He really did make the atonement a fulfilled reality for all eternity. Satan won a victory over Eve and Adam and mankind so many centuries before. Satan spoiled the creation with his vandalism, and all nature became abnormal. In the book of Romans Paul tells us (Romans 8:22) that the whole of creation groans and is in pain, waiting for the final redemption. *Now* the moment which is still ahead, is being glimpsed by John, and by us! For joined to the angel voices, next John hears, "And every created thing which is in heaven and on the earth and under the earth, and such as are in the sea and all that are in them, heard I saying, Blessing, and honor, and glory, and power be unto him that sitteth upon the throne, and unto the *Lamb* forever and ever ... and the four and twenty elders fell down and worshiped him that liveth forever and ever."

Yes, all nature will praise the Lamb for what He has been willing to do to restore nature to have a victory which wipes out the chaos left by the vandal's work. The Lamb has been victorious!

EIGHTEEN

Even if this was all that John was shown, think what it would mean to him as he had the memory of Nero's ghastly tortures, of Titus's horrible devastation of Jerusalem, of the suffering of persecuted Christians being thrown to the lions, all still very fresh in his mind. Think of how eager John would be to get this all down, to write just what God wanted him to record for all who would be born in years to come, before Jesus would come back! John might have been on a rocky island washed by waves, but he was not separated from his memories, nor could he forget that his exile there was a concentration camp type of experience. He had difficult times still ahead. Oh, what a moment of realization that final victory is ahead, and an eternity of joy, before he went back to suffer, and to write!

But there is much more. The Lamb is opening seals to show what is ahead, and the fifth seal opens to John's vision the souls of those who have been martyred for the testimony of God (Revelation 6:9-16). These martyrs are crying with a loud voice saying, "How long, O Lord, holy and true, before you will judge and avenge our blood...." And John saw white robes given them, and heard them told that they should rest for a time, until the very last ones, their brethren (brethren in the family of the Lord, and fellow martyrs for the truth) would also be killed. *Then* will come the day of the Lamb's wrath. The meek and mild Jesus, the Lamb who stood dumb before false accusation, the One who allowed Himself to be killed so that He could be the substitute, will be the Judge. Kings, leaders, rich men, powerful men, captains and mighty people, as well as bondsmen, will suddenly recognize that they cannot stand against His judgment, and they will try to flee to rocks and caves to get away from "the wrath of the Lamb." "For the great day of his wrath is come; and who shall be able to stand?"

It is not the God of the Old Testament, the God of Abraham, Isaac, and David, who is "harsh" as some people seem to think and teach, and that Jesus is to be contrasted to Him as gentle and understanding. The Triune God is One. God the Father is gentle and understanding and compassionate and full of love, as Jesus is. But The Lamb, Jesus the Messiah, is holy, and is just, as God the Father is. The Lamb will be the Judge. The

One who died to make forgiveness possible to every one who believes will judge those who have turned away to believe Satan, and have not been seeking with all their hearts. The pragmatic governments of the world have no "absolute" as a base, and suddenly men who have been doing what other men have been doing get "caught" and judgment is meted out. So often the judges are not better than the ones judged.

The Lamb is different. Jesus, the Second Person of the Trinity, the Messiah, is different. He is perfect. He is without sin. He took the sin of others upon himself, and went through all that was necessary to give free pardon. This is not an arbitrary decision. This is not a "winking" at broken law and sin. The *way* was opened in the beginning before the "curse" was spelled out. Now the *way* has been accomplished and opened for centuries before His return. There has been time enough for people to find out, before the last martyr is killed by the last hateful scoffer, and the Lamb becomes the Judge.

We fly on to chapter seven and find that with John we are seeing twelve thousand from each of the twelve tribes of Israel gathered together, and in addition a "great multitude which no man could number" of all nations and kindreds, and people, and tongues standing before the throne and before the *Lamb,* clothed with white robes, and holding palms in their hands. And they cry with a loud voice, saying, "Salvation to our God which sitteth upon the throne, and unto the Lamb."

Tribes of Israel? Yes they are named. From each tribe there are gathered 12,000 in this special grouping, making 144,000 in all. Each tribe is named, Juda, Reuben, Gad, Aser, Nepthalim, Manasses, Simeon, Levi, Issachar, Zabulon, Joseph, Benjamin. Are these *all* the Jews who will be there? No, when the elder asked John who all these people were, John replied, "Sir, thou knowest," so the elder told him, "These are they which came out of great tribulation and have washed their robes and made them white in the blood of the *Lamb."* There is a special time of great tribulation which will be imposed by the anti-Christ who will be anti-Semitic to the extreme, and during this period there will be this special number "sealed" by their trust in the Lamb.

EIGHTEEN

How thrilling to find that the combined number from all nations and kindreds and people and tongues—with no color, language, family line, nation, excluded; no caste system here, no ghetto portions of the city here, no front and back seats here—that this combined number is *more* than man can number, a great multitude! This great multitude will be arrayed in white robes, and they will be before the throne of God, and what promises are there for their fulfillment?

"They shall hunger no more, neither thirst anymore...." No more hunger, no famine, no lack of water, no shortages! Ah, but man shall not live by bread alone, so this covers more than fulfilling physical food, there shall be no hunger and thirst for communication, love, joy, peace, and all the things we are capable of needing and capable of having fulfilled. There will be enough for everyone emotionally, spiritually, intellectually. God who made man in His image knows what is needed, and plans in the place of eternity to fulfill all the needs.

"For the Lamb which is in the midst of the throne shall feed them [yes, the Lamb is the bread of life forever now] and shall lead them into living fountains of waters [this same One who spoke to the woman at the well and said He would give water that would quench thirst forever, is now fulfilling that promise] and God shall wipe all tears from their eyes."

Do we understand perfectly? No, but we *do* understand *something*. No human being could pick up such writing and read it without understanding something, unless he had been brainwashed to think that there is no such thing as truth, and no such thing as a "future." No more tears does not mean tear glands stopped up. "God wiping all tears from their eyes" does not mean a continual weeping with God using a linen cloth to continually wipe. It is clear that the sorrow and suffering which causes weeping will be removed, and that there will be so much peace, joy, gentleness, love, appreciation, kindness, fulfillment, discovery, understanding, supply of every need, that the tears of anger, sorrow, suffering, frustration, disappointment, will not be needed. Tears will be gone.

We swoop down to the universe-shaking scene being shown us in chapter twelve. Here we need to remember that Satan has

been going before God and *accusing* the people of God's
family, the believers, the brethren who are brothers because
they have all been born the second time into one family. Of *what*
has Satan been accusing the people of God? The book of Job
tells us that Satan tells God something like this: "Job doesn't
love *you,* he loves his health, family, wealth, lands, house,
animals and so forth. Just let him lose some of these things and
you will see." It is *that* kind of statement Satan has been
making for centuries about all of God's people. And in
every kind of circumstance Satan has attacked God through
hitting at God's people, until finally, I believe, the possibilities
will be all finished. Satan will have tried everything, and it will
have been proved that what God said to Paul, "My grace is
sufficient for thee for my strength is made perfect in
weakness," was not only true for Paul with his thorn in the flesh,
but has been true of each of God's children in a variety of
circumstances. The victory Christ died to make possible is
also in the realm of victory over the temptation to stop
trusting and loving God. Each child of God in the midst of
suffering has had some small part in completing the finished
tapestry of victory! It will be interesting to trace the different
threads!

Now comes the long-waited-for moment, the moment for
which angels and martyrs have waited so breathlessly! What a
moment for Michael and the angels as they get the task of
tossing Satan and his demons out ... never, *never* again to
accuse anyone before God! That will be finished then! I
wonder who will be the last person accused, and in what sort of
circumstance.

Let me quote what God gave John to write so that we may
be sure of this future moment: "And there was a war in heaven:
Michael and his angels fought against the dragon; and the dragon
fought and his angels, and prevailed not; neither was their
place found any more in heaven. And the great dragon was
cast out, that old serpent, called the Devil and Satan, which
deceiveth the whole world: he was cast out into the earth, and his
angels were cast out with him. And I heard a loud voice saying
in heaven, Now is come salvation and strength, and the

EIGHTEEN

kingdom of our God, and the power of his Christ: for the *accuser of our brethren is cast down,* which accused them before our God day and night" (Revelation 12:7-10).

It is finished! He can't do it any more! His destructive work of trying to separate God from the love and trust of His own people, is over! The relationship of God's family with their Father can now go on without interruption. However, the opportunity of *proving* to God that we love Him best and not our health, comfort, rest, ease, material possessions, power, and men's praise, will also be over at the same time. One thing we need to be aware of right now is that this future time will one day be here, then we can't say, "Wait a minute, I want to prove something first: I love you, and I'll do anything for you, Lord."

We await a marvelous moment which *will* arrive as each moment God has told us about will arrive. But in our excitement of looking forward, it is important not to forget the meaning of the historic reality to God of what we have to give Him right now.

How can we possibly *not* fall into Satan's trap and murmur and complain daily against God? Verse 11 tells *how* anyone has had victory over Satan, who has ever had such a victory: "And they overcame him by the blood of the Lamb, and by the word of their testimony; and they loved not their lives unto the death." Before Jesus came and died, Abraham, Isaac, Jacob, Joseph, Daniel, David, as well as Stephen, Peter, Paul, they all overcame by the blood of the Lamb, and they loved the Lord more than their own lives. "And if not ... we will still not worship your image, O king...." Hear the men as they braved the fate of burning in the furnace ... they loved God more than their lives, as the martyrs throughout the centuries have done. Each one has "overcome by the blood of the Lamb," whether they lived on the A.D. side of the cross or the B.C. side of the cross. There is a unity here among all of God's children from Abel who was killed by Cain for worshiping correctly and so was the first martyr, right up to the last martyr—whoever that is to be. Jews and Gentiles, each one who loves the living God, has shown forth that love, through the power and victory *given* to them, which was "paid for" by the atonement the *Lamb* did die to make possible.

The overcoming of Satan's attacks against God through God's people, is important. The proving of a restored communication with God as we pray and have answers is also important. There are two kinds of victory which will no longer be needed when the battle is over, and there is no longer anything to "overcome"! That will be a time of peace which will be *real* peace, and not just peace written in papers while the smoke of embassy buildings is still darkening the sky, not just peace written on a "United Nations" building while the nations send battleships into each other's waters. The final peace which will come when the final victory is won and the enemy is cast out, will be a solid peace.

But there is more our bird's flight must pass over, before dipping down again to listen to another song being sung after another victory, and it is a very fantastic combination of words and music called the Song of Moses and the Lamb! Yes, Moses, who told the people of Israel how to prepare the first passover lamb, seems to have a song combined with the song of The Lamb who fulfilled all the passovers. John puts it this way: "And they sing the song of Moses the servant of God, and the song of the Lamb, saying, Great and marvelous are thy works, Lord God Almighty; just and true are thy ways, thou King of saints."

Perhaps you have heard this song sung, or perhaps you have sung it yourself. Did you know that John wrote it down in Revelation 15:3 and that it was called the Song of Moses and the Lamb?

Look at the continuity! The crescendo of continuity is like hearing the final movement of a symphony in which all the parts are coming together. Notes are there you heard early in the music, instruments are now being combined to come to the final, gorgeous, blending conclusion. The marvel of the end of the Bible is that it is not an end, but a beginning. But there is no doubt that the beginning is based on all past history. What is ahead is not disconnected. History has an effect into the future. Ripples go out to be lost in the horizon, though they are still there: Moses, the Lamb, the people who have come through the centuries—more than can be numbered—they are there, they matter.

Smooth your feathers, O bird; take us gently down to view what John saw in his vision, and which we are to see one day too when it takes place truly, in the moment being reserved in future history. Time reserved—for a wedding, and a wedding supper! We float now over this scene as the voices thunder up saying, "Alleluia." "And I heard as it were the voice of a great multitude and as the voice of many waters, and as the voice of mighty thunderings, [have you been at the seaside during a storm and heard the thunder vie with the crash of the waves?] saying, Alleluia: for the Lord God omnipotent reigneth. Let us be glad and rejoice, and give honor to him: for the marriage of the *Lamb* is come, and his wife hath made herself ready."

The marriage of the Lamb? Yes, the Lamb is not only our Shepherd, our King, our Savior, our Messiah, but He is our bridegroom. Paul makes clear to the Ephesians in his letter to them that Christ is the bridegroom of the church, and that even as man and wife became physically one, Christ and the church (remember that means all those who are believers, Jews and Gentiles alike) are spiritually one. What is "the bride" to wear for this occasion? John goes on to tell us what he was shown: "And to her was granted that she should be arrayed in fine linen, clean and white, for the fine linen is the righteousness of saints."

White? But that is for purity, and this "bride" is made up of thousands upon thousands of sinners from every century, now combined in one people. How could white be appropriate? Ah, but this is the fantastic reality being clearly portrayed now as we all receive our crisp white linen robes designed by the One who designed the flowers—this One, who made the white roses, white orchids, white daisies, white chrysanthemums, white violets! These white robes are to portray a very specific thing: we are *covered* with the righteousness of the Lamb who died to take our place. His death was for our sins, so the filthy rags we had on us, made up of our sins, He took in exchange, and now very literally He gives us the outward demonstration to put on, which speaks forth to all who will see, that *His righteousness* has been given to His bride, every single person who has accepted Him as Messiah and Savior!

Our detail-perfect God will fulfill the details which make the picture perfect ... in the future, even as He has in the past. Our righteousness is *His* righteousness given to us, and we shall wear clothing to this wedding supper which will make us very conscious of this having taken place. No person will need to be afraid of a spot or blemish, as it is *His* whiteness given to cover us. We need not tremble that some sinful spot is going to show up! He has washed us clean, and in addition will give us the prepared clothing of His perfection.

"And he saith unto me, Write, Blessed are they which are called unto the marriage supper of the Lamb. And he saith unto me, These things are the true sayings of God."

Do you remember that in the time Jesus was having the last passover with His disciples, and the first communion, that He said, "I say unto you I will not any more eat thereof until it be fulfilled in the kingdom of God... And he took the cup, and gave thanks and said, Take this, and divide it among yourselves, for I say unto you I will not drink of the fruit of the vine until the kingdom of God shall come."

Now John is being shown, and is telling us, that the literal reality of what Jesus spoke of is going to take place in a future moment of history. The bride, dressed for the occasion, will sit down and have a wedding supper. The bread and fruit of the vine will be given by the Lamb, the Bridegroom, to the bride, and history will be gathered together in memory, all the way back to the passover lamb, through the centuries following and on up to the time when the Lamb of God died and left "the Lord's supper" as a manner of looking back and forward. The time has come when everything is behind and even as a bride leaves her home to start a new life, this "bride of the Lamb," the people of God, the sheep of his flock, will leave behind the life of the full history of the world, and step into an entirely new home, and new life. The wedding supper is an ending, and a beginning.

EIGHTEEN

After the supper the angel is seen to bind Satan up for a thousand years, and then will begin the time which Daniel tells about, when the lion will lie down with the little lambs, and snakes will no longer be poisonous, and wars will cease, and men will see what a perfectly just ruler will be like. Christ will be King, the promised ruler of Israel, living and reigning a thousand years. This millennium time is often quoted on men's walls of "utopian buildings" planned to house the peace plans of men. But at this time there really will be pruning hooks made out of the implements of war, and nature will be lush and beautiful without the blights. The anti-Christ who has been dictator during a terrible time of tribulation will have been overthrown; and the earth will be freed of Satan's attacks for this period of time.

We are on our way up a mountain with John now as one of the angels carries John up to see the city where the "bride" will live. This is the city prepared by the Father, who has no need to be ashamed as each one will have a place ready.

"And he carried me away in the spirit to a great and high mountain, and showed me that great city, the holy Jerusalem, descending out of heaven from God, having the glory of God: and her light was like a stone most precious, even like a jasper stone, clear as crystal" (Revelation 21:10-27).

Like a planet this beautiful Jerusalem descends into John's view, and ours as we look with him. An amazing city, foursquare, with its foundation as wonderful as its buildings. But look closely—there is a combining, a blending, a weaving together of history in the gates and the foundations. There are names on the gates, these gates made each of one gigantic pearl. The names are the names of the twelve tribes of Israel! Jewish gates to the heavenly Jerusalem. But of course—it is the promised land, promised so long ago, now in complete fulfillment. The high walls are jasper stone and the city is of pure gold, like unto clear glass. John could find no description closer than transparent gold to help us "see" this marvelous building material indirectly lighted. He tells of the length and breadth and width of it all, and it measures about 1400 miles cubed. A breathtaking sight indeed.

It floats in space, and we approach it as men approach the moon. We see that the foundations are filled with the beauty of precious stones which are named, all twelve of them, stones like emerald, topaz, amethyst. Twelve? Yes, there are twelve stones, different for each foundation, and in the foundations are the names of the twelve Apostles. So the Old Testament is represented by the twelve tribes of Israel named on the gates, and the New Testament is represented by the twelve Apostles named in the foundations. Do you want to know something amazing? Every one of those people named is a Jew. How can anyone say Christianity is anything but Jewish? What about the Gentiles? Don't you remember that every single person coming to live in this city has been "born again"—and that the second birth makes each one a spiritual child of Abraham, as well as a child of the living God? It is *one* family, and we are *all* represented by the twelve tribes and the twelve Apostles, every tribe, and nation, and kindred and tongue and people have some representatives there. Each one *belongs.*

Is there a Temple in this Jerusalem? No. Why not? Why no Temple for worship in the heavenly Jerusalem? Isn't the Temple the center of life with God? Listen carefully to what God gave John to tell us: "And I saw no temple therein, for the Lord God Almighty and the *Lamb* are the temple of it." There is no Temple built by men's hands; the Temple was the dwelling place of God among men on earth at one period of time. Now all who are God's children are in *His dwelling place.* He *is* the Temple, and the Lamb is the temple—we dwell together forever.

For a moment *please* put yourself in the place of a person who has lived in the slums of the most polluted city in the world. Put yourself in the place of a person sitting on ragged scraps as their only "house" with no cover to protect them from flies or heat or cold. Put yourself in the place of a person who has never seen a clean, light, beautiful home in his or her whole existence, who has never eaten pleasant food, nor felt soft, clean beauty, nor been presented with a gift of any sort, and has never known kindness. Then imagine trying to understand a description of an opposite kind of situation. Imagine trying to understand a description of the Swiss Alps, at sunrise or sunset, with the most delicious of food set on delicately perfect china, spread on a marvelously crisp, beautiful tablecloth—with an orchestra playing the most beautiful music that you could not imagine because you had never seen or heard an orchestra. Try to imagine sitting in your filth and squalor and feeling a reality about a description of the most wonderful combination of things in this world's nature and possible gifts of things to see, smell, taste, feel, and hear. Could it easily be made *real*?

This is where we are as we listen and consider what God is telling us through John. It is only a partial description He is giving us of a small fraction of all that is ahead, but it is a glimpse of something *real*. God, who attends to details throughout all history, is not describing *more* than exists, but is promising that it will be the other way around. "Eye hath not seen, nor ear heard, neither have entered into the heart of man, the things which God hath prepared for them that love him."

What is ahead is beyond description, and beyond our imagination because we have nothing with which to compare it; we have not experienced anything that has *not* been spoiled by sin. Everything we have known—the most "perfect" moments—carry some element of disappointment because no person is perfect, no circumstance is without a flaw. There is no perfect control of conditions, government decisions, snipers, hijackers, strikes, fires, earthquakes, hail, stormy floods and high seas, illness, and accident. Crushed hopes and broken promises men know very much about, but perfection is beyond them. How can God tell us?

Ah, but listen. Listen to the clear trumpet tones, the blend of violin and cello, French horns and strong piano, tinkling triangle and bass drums, violas and pure recorder notes, high flute and deep bassoons—listen to the blend of all the sounds you have ever known, and more you must imagine. Feel, with all the emotion you have in your constitution, and realize you will need to have more than you have ever known. Taste with memory of tastes but imagine new taste buds necessary to discern the difference of ambrosia from earthly tastes. Think with all the brain power you have, and realize that perfection will give you clarity of thought you have never known before, beside which all your thoughts will seem like a muddy stream. See in imagination the difference between seeing through a muddied-up glass, seeing vandalized art work, and suddenly seeing perfection. Try to put aside all the preconceptions that take away any possibility of being honest and then read what God gave John next to describe for our *hope:* "And the city had no need of the sun, neither of the moon to shine in it: for the glory of God did lighten it, and the Lamb is the light thereof."

Paul on the Damascus Road had fallen to his face before the light of the risen Lord as He appeared to him. Just a short time before, John had fallen flat before the stunning light and glory of Jesus as he spoke to him there on Patmos. The *light* of the heavenly city is this glorious light of the glory of God—no other light is needed. "And the *Lamb* is the light thereof." We need not get lost; we *know* who this is—the Lamb who is our Shepherd, who has been praying for us every day, every moment in His intercession as High Priest, is the *light*. What light to look forward to as we walk in a world filled with gross darkness! Can we imagine light without darkness?

"And the gates of it shall not be shut at all by day: for there is no night there." No locked gates, no night—there will be coming and going, in and out. We are told so. Gates, twelve of them, and other places to go to from this heavenly city. Can you imagine that God—who made man in his own image, to be able to think and act and feel, to choose and create in so many areas—when He removes the curse and gives us perfection without hindrance, will provide *less* in the areas of study, discovery, and understanding? Everything given to us points to more, more, *more.* Can we think men can do more *now* in the way of research, discovery, invention, creative arts, than they can do when sin and Satan's attacks are removed? The problem is that people have refused to believe God, but God has told them—and there is no excuse.

We are next told that *nothing* will enter into this city that defileth it. Does that exclude us, as sinners? No, because we have been cleansed, and the spotless righteousness of the Messiah has been given to us, and we are correctly clothed, covered now forever, with our sins removed as far as the east is from the west. And we are told here that as each of us believes, his or her name is recorded. Listen: "... but they which are written in the *Lamb's* book of life." The Lamb paid a very expensive price for the names to be written in this book, so in a totally real way it is *His* book. This is the book in which every name written has everlasting life because He died on the cross to make the book possible. What a precious book to the Lamb! It is a precious book to us also because it records the moment of our "birth"—our birth into Abraham's line, his family, and God's. No one's name who accepts what Christ the Messiah has done for him or her, will be left out. There are no mistakes made.

Is that all? No, there is one more chapter in the Bible, and our bird's flight must hover over this until we have had a good glimpse.

There is water there, called the river of the water of life. It is described as being "clear as crystal," because we have no more words to help us see its beauty than John had from God. We know something of sparkling crystal if we have seen it; this is water coming from "the throne of God and of the *Lamb*." Yes, there is a throne, and a tumbling, sparkling river of the water of life, and the *Lamb* is on the throne beside God the Father.

The streets are of gold like transparent glass, although when we see them we will have a richer vocabulary with which to describe them. There is a street in the middle, and the river flows down the middle of the city also, with a grove of trees on either side, or is it just two trees? Ezekiel 47:12 speaks of trees whose leaf shall not fade and which produce new fruit according to the months because of the special water. John tells us in this last chapter: "... on either side of the river, was there the tree of life, which bare twelve manner of fruits, and yielded her fruit every month."

Fantastic trees and real fruit, but we only understand in part right now. It is sufficient, however, to make us excited about it, unless we are dull, drab, unimaginative people with our heads hung down, never looking at all at what we have been given.

Lest we are in doubt about all the perfection, it is re-emphasized and spelled out for us: "And there shall be *no more curse;* but the throne of God and of the *Lamb* shall be in it; and his servants shall serve him: And they shall see his face...."

Oh, what restoration! Adam and Eve walked in the cool of the day with God, communicating, enjoying His perfect creation, full of ideas as to what to name the animals, caring for the marvelously landscaped garden with no sweat and tears. Centuries and centuries of spoiledness followed, with the "curse" changing all that, and with man never to see "face to face" in all that time, as people will be "seeing his face" in that heavenly city. It is the restoration that is beyond our imaginations. God the Creator who made everything has promised that He is preparing all this, and more!

Do we believe *Him?* Blessed are they, said Jesus, who have *not* seen, and yet who believe. We have been given enough to believe to be very blessed! One day we shall see, feel, taste, smell, understand—and it will be too late to believe without seeing!

In case each of us asks what God knows we *may* ask, the answer is given next. First we are told again that there will be no night there, and no need of candle or sun because the Lord God will give us light, and we shall reign forever and ever. We will have *all* the light we need, spiritual light to understand, intellectual light to understand, physical light to "see" in every detail what He has prepared for us, and it will not be temporary, it will be everlasting, forever and forever, and ever and ever.

Is there any more? Yes, that answer to any doubt: "These sayings are faithful and *true:* and the Lord God of the holy prophets [what prophets?—Isaiah, Jeremiah, Ezekiel, Daniel, Hosea, Jonah, Amos ... all those Jewish prophets] sent *His* angel to shew unto His servants the things which must be done shortly."

EIGHTEEN

How much more strongly can God connect history with the everlasting life in the future? How much more strongly can He tell us it is *"true,"* that all that has been given us in His Word is true? Satan hates anyone believing that truth even exists, let alone that God has spoken truth. The choice is before us; whom will we believe? The center of attack today is against *truth*.

How does the Bible end after this? And now to the end of our flight:

It is reiterated that the Messiah, the Alpha and Omega, will *come* again, will come quickly. We are told we can have total confidence in what has been told us and the last six verses of the Bible are like a rising crescendo of sound, with blasts of trumpets blown by tall, straight, beautiful trumpeters. "I, Jesus, have sent my angel to testify unto you these things.... I am the root and offspring of David, the bright and morning star." Any doubt about who is speaking? The promised *One,* promised to Abraham, is binding it all up and handing it to us, so that we can have confidence that it is true.

An invitation is next—the last invitation of the Bible: "And the Spirit [that is, the Holy Spirit, the Third Person of the Trinity] and the bride [that is the bride of Christ, the bride of the Lamb ... made up of all believers] say, *come.*... And let him that heareth say *come.* And let him that is athirst *come.* And *whosoever will* let him take of the water of life freely."

Can we give and receive and believe such a gorgeous invitation to *come* to Him and accept what He has done for us?

Please, please wipe everything else out of your mind now, and let us listen to the final *warning* of the Word of God. Eve and Adam did not heed the warning given in the beginning. Eve and Adam went diametrically against that first warning of God. Oh, now don't say you haven't heard his *last* warning, because here it is—in the very last verse of the Bible. "For I testify unto every man that heareth the words of the prophecy of this book. [That refers to me, to you, to anyone who is now hearing.] ... if any man shall *add* unto these things, God shall add unto him the plagues that are written in this book."

That is the first solemn, clear warning, introduced by a blast of trumpets: Don't add anything. Don't add requirements God has not given. Don't add ways of coming to Him that He hasn't given. Don't add a list of "do's" or "don'ts" that He has not given. This is serious. To add to God's Word is to set oneself up as telling God He has not had a high enough standard, it is a putting of oneself above God.

The second solemn warning? What is there left to warn about? "And if any man shall take away from the words of the book of this prophecy, God shall take away his part out of the book of life, and out of the holy city, and from the things which are written in this book."

Scissors cutting the Bible to shreds? Erasers erasing part of the book of Revelation? Sneers which intimidate people into shrugging it all off? How are we in danger of the unbelief which rips God's Word into pieces and calls *Him* a liar? The last warning is the same as the warning given to Eve and Adam. God said, "*If* ... then the following will happen." Now His Word is more complete ... it is contained in the whole book. The warning is as emphatic and drastic. Who is going to toss away the lessons all history has been teaching? Centuries of demonstration. Centuries of examples. Now a verbalized warning to cap it off: Be warned. Re-read, and remember what God has said.

Who has said this? The very last short two verses identify the speaker again: "He which testifieth these things saith, Surely I come quickly: Amen. Even so *come,* Lord Jesus. The grace of our Lord Jesus Christ be with you, Amen." It is the One promised to Eve and Adam who is speaking, the One promised to Abraham, the One who came to give victory over Satan's attack—the Old Testament-prophesied Messiah—and the One who fulfilled all the promises.

Don't shut the book and walk away. You have read what the Alpha and Omega gives as an authentic invitation. A reply is expected!